LEONARD COHEN

Book of Longing

PENGUIN BOOKS

PENGUIN BOOKS

Published by the Penguin Group
Penguin Books Ltd, 80 Strand, London WC2R 0RL, England
Penguin Group (USA) Inc., 375 Hudson Street, New York, New York 10014, USA
Penguin Group (Canada), 90 Eglinton Avenue East, Suite 700, Toronto, Ontario, Canada M4P 2Y3
(a division of Pearson Penguin Canada Inc.)
Penguin Ireland, 25 St Stephen's Green, Dublin 2, Ireland (a division of Penguin Books Ltd)
Penguin Group (Australia), 250 Camberwell Road,
Camberwell, Victoria 3124, Australia (a division of Pearson Australia Group Pty Ltd)
Penguin Books India Pvt Ltd, 11 Community Centre, Panchsheel Park, New Delhi – 110 017, India
Penguin Group (NZ), 67 Apollo Drive, Rosedale, North Shore 0632,
Auckland 1310, New Zealand (a division of Pearson New Zealand Ltd)
Penguin Books (South Africa) (Pty) Ltd, 24 Sturdee Avenue, Rosebank, Johannesburg 2196, South Africa

Penguin Books Ltd, Registered Offices: 80 Strand, London WC2R 0RL, England

www.penguin.com

First published in Canada by McClelland & Stewart Ltd. 2006
First published in Great Britain by Viking 2006
Published in Penguin Books 2007

1

We acknowledge the financial support of the Government of Canada through the
Book Publishing Industry Development Program and that of the Government of Ontario
through the Ontario Media Development Corporation's Ontario Book Initiative.
We further acknowledge the support of the Canada Council for the Arts and the
Ontario Arts Council for our publishing program.

Printed in England by Clays Ltd, St Ives plc

ISBN: 978–0–141–02756–2

www.greenpenguin.co.uk

Mixed Sources
Product group from well managed
forests and other controlled sources
www.fsc.org Cert no. SA-COC-1592
© 1996 Forest Stewardship Council

Penguin Books is committed to a sustainable future
for our business, our readers and our planet.
The book in your hands is made from paper
certified by the Forest Stewardship Council.

for Irving Layton

Book of Longing

THE BOOK OF LONGING

I can't make the hills
The system is shot
I'm living on pills
For which I thank G-d

I followed the course
From chaos to art
Desire the horse
Depression the cart

I sailed like a swan
I sank like a rock
But time is long gone
Past my laughing stock

My page was too white
My ink was too thin
The day wouldn't write
What the night pencilled in

My animal howls
My angel's upset
But I'm not allowed
A trace of regret

For someone will use
What I couldn't be
My heart will be hers
Impersonally

She'll step on the path
She'll see what I mean
My will cut in half
And freedom between

For less than a second
Our lives will collide
The endless suspended
The door open wide

Then she will be born
To someone like you
What no one has done
She'll continue to do

I know she is coming
I know she will look
And that is the longing
And this is the book

My Life in Robes

After a while
You can't tell
If it's missing
A woman
Or needing
A cigarette
And later on
If it's night
Or day
Then suddenly
You know
The time
You get dressed
You go home
You light up
You get married

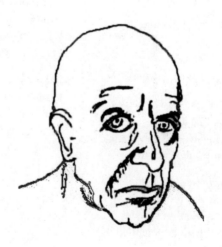

HIS MASTER'S VOICE

After listening to Mozart
(which I often did)
I would always
Carry a piano
Up and down
Mt. Baldy
And I don't mean
A keyboard
I mean a full-sized
Grand piano
Made of cement
Now that I am dying
I don't regret
A single step

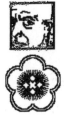

ROSHI AT 89

Roshi's very tired,
> he's lying on his bed
He's been living with the living
> and dying with the dead
But now he wants another drink
> (will wonders never cease?)
He's making war on war
> and he's making war on peace
He's sitting in the throne-room
> on his great Original Face
and he's making war on Nothing
> that has Something in its place
His stomach's very happy
> The prunes are working well
There's no one going to Heaven
> and there's no one left in Hell

– Mt. Baldy, 1996

ONE OF MY LETTERS

I corresponded with a famous rabbi
but my teacher caught sight of one of my letters
and silenced me.
"Dear Rabbi," I wrote him for the last time,
"I do not have the authority or understanding
to speak of these matters.
I was just showing off.
Please forgive me.
Your Jewish brother,
Jikan Eliezer."

YOU'D SING TOO

You'd sing too
if you found yourself
in a place like this
You wouldn't worry about
whether you were as good
as Ray Charles or Edith Piaf
You'd sing
You'd sing
not for yourself
but to make a self
out of the old food
rotting in the astral bowel
and the loveless thud
of your own breathing
You'd become a singer
faster than it takes
to hate a rival's charm
and you'd sing, darling
you'd sing too

S.O.S. 1995

Take a long time with your anger,
sleepyhead.
Don't waste it in riots.
Don't tangle it with ideas.
The Devil won't let me speak,
will only let me hint
that you are a slave,
your misery a deliberate policy
of those in whose thrall you suffer,
and who are sustained
by your misfortune.
The atrocities over there,
the interior paralysis over here –
Pleased with the better deal?
You are clamped down.
You are being bred for pain.
The Devil ties my tongue.
I'm speaking to you,
'friend of my scribbled life.'
You have been conquered by those
who know how to conquer invisibly.
The curtains move so beautifully,
lace curtains of some
sweet old intrigue:
the Devil tempting me
to turn away from alarming you.

So I must say it quickly:
Whoever is in your life,
those who harm you,
those who help you;
those whom you know
and those whom you do not know –
let them off the hook,
help them off the hook.
Recognize the hook.
You are listening to Radio Resistance.

WHEN I DRINK

When I drink
the $300 scotch
with Roshi
it quenches every thirst
A song comes to my lips
a woman lies down with me
and every desire
invites me to curl up naked
in its dripping jaws

No more, I cry, no more
but Roshi fills my glass again
and new passions consume me
new appetites
For instance
I fall into a tulip
(and never hit the bottom)
or I hurtle through the night
in sweaty sexual union
with someone about twice the size
of the Big Dipper

When I eat meat with Roshi
the four-legged animals
don't cry any more
and the two-legged animals
don't try to fly away
and the exhausted salmon
come home to my hand
and Roshi's wolf
biting at its broken chain
creates a sensation
in the cabin
by making friends with everyone

When I chow down with Roshi
and the Ballantine flows
the pine trees inch into my bosom
the great boring grey boulders
of Mt. Baldy
creep into my heart
and they all get fed
with the delicious fat
and the white cheese popcorn
or whatever it is
they've wanted all these years

BETTER

better than darkness
is fake darkness
which swindles you
into necking with
someone's antique
cousin

better than banks
are false banks
where you change
all your rough money
into legal tender

better than coffee
is blue coffee
which you drink
in your last bath
or sometimes waiting
for your shoes
to be dismantled

better than poetry
is my poetry
which refers
to everything
that is beautiful and
dignified, but is
neither of these itself

better than wild
is secretly wild
as when I am in
the darkness of
a parking space
with a new snake

better than art
is repulsive art
which demonstrates
better than scripture
the tiny measure
of your improvement

better than darkness
is darkless
which is inkier, vaster
more profound
and eerily refrigerated
filled with caves
and blinding tunnels
in which appear
beckoning dead relatives
and other religious
paraphernalia

better than love
is wuve
which is more refined
superbly erotic
tiny serene people
with huge genitalia
but lighter than thought
comfortably installed
on an eyelash of mist
and living grimly
ever after
cooking, gardening
and raising kids

better than my mother
is your mother
who is still alive
while mine
is not alive
but what am I saying!
forgive me mother

better than me
are you
kinder than me
are you
sweeter smarter faster
you you you
prettier than me
stronger than me
lonelier than me

I want to get
to know you
better and better

    – Mt. Baldy, 1996

THE LOVESICK MONK

I shaved my head
I put on robes
I sleep in the corner of a cabin
sixty-five hundred feet up a mountain
It's dismal here
The only thing I don't need
is a comb

– Mt. Baldy, 1997

TO A YOUNG NUN

This undemanding love
that our staggered births
have purchased for us –
You in your generation,
I in mine.
I am not the one
you are looking for.
You are not the one
I've stopped looking for.
How sweetly time
disposes of us
as we go arm in arm
over the Bridge of Details:
Your turn to chop.
My turn to cook.
Your turn to die for love.
My turn to resurrect.

OTHER WRITERS

Steve Sanfield is a great haiku master.
He lives in the country with Sarah,
his beautiful wife,
and he writes about the small things
which stand for all things.
Kyozan Joshu Roshi,
who has brought hundreds of monks
to a full awakening,
addresses the simultaneous
expansion and contraction
of the cosmos.
I go on and on
about a noble young woman
who unfastened her jeans
in the front seat of my jeep
and let me touch
the source of life
because I was so far from it.
I've got to tell you, friends,
I prefer my stuff to theirs.

ROSHI

I never really understood
what he said
but every now and then
I find myself
barking with the dog
or bending with the irises
or helping out
in other little ways

MEDICINE

My medicine
Has many contrasting flavours.
Engrossed in, or perplexed by
The differences between them,
The patient forgets to suffer.

TRUE SELF

True Self, True Self
has no will –
It's free from "Kill"
or "Do not kill"
but while I am
a novice still
I do embrace
with all my will
the First Commitment
"Do not kill"

THE COLLAPSE OF ZEN

When I can wedge my face
into the place
and struggle with my breathing
as she brings her eager fingers down
        to separate herself,
to help me use my whole mouth
against her hungriness,
        her most private of hungers –
why should I want to be enlightened?
Is there something that I missed?
Have I forgotten yesterday's mosquito
or tomorrow's hungry ghost?

When I can roam this hill with a knife in my back
caused by too much drinking of Chateau Latour
and spill my heart into the valley
        of the lights of Caguas
and freeze in fear as the watchdog
comes drooling out of the bushes
and refuses to recognize me
and there we are, yes, bewildered
as to who should kill the other first –
and I move and it moves,
and it moves and I move,
why should I want to be enlightened?
Did I leave something out?
Was there some world I failed to embrace?
Some bone I didn't steal?

When Jesus loves me so much that blood
        comes out of his heart
and I climb a metal ladder
into the hole in his bosom
which is caused by sorrow as big as China
and I enter the innermost room wearing white clothes

and I entreat and I plead:
"Not this one, Sir. Not that one, Sir. I beg you, Sir."
and I look through His eyes
as the helpless are shit on again
and the tender blooming nipple of mankind
is caught in the pincers
of power and muscle and money –
why should I seek enlightenment?
Did I fail to recognize some cockroach?
Some vermin in the ooze of my majesty?

When 'men are stupid and women are crazy'
and everyone is asleep in San Juan and Caguas
and everyone is in love but me
and everyone has a religion and a boyfriend
and a great genius for loneliness –

When I can dribble over all the universes
and undress a woman without touching her
and run errands for my urine
        and offer my huge silver shoulders
to the pinhead moon –
When my heart is broken as usual
over someone's evanescent beauty
and design after design
they fade like kingdoms with no writing
and, look, I wheeze my way
up to the station of Sahara's
        incomparable privacy
and churn the air into a dark cocoon
of effortless forgetting –
why should I shiver on the altar of enlightenment?
why should I want to smile forever?

EARLY MORNING AT MT. BALDY

Alarm awakened me at 2:30 a.m.:
got into my robes
kimono and *hakama*
modelled after the 12th-century
archer's costume:
on top of this the *koroma*
a heavy outer garment
with impossibly large sleeves:
on top of this the *ruksu*
a kind of patchwork bib
which incorporates an ivory disc:
and finally the four-foot
serpentine belt
that twists into a huge handsome knot
resembling a braided *challah*
and covers the bottom of the *ruksu*:
all in all
about 20 pounds of clothing
which I put on quickly
at 2:30 a.m.
over my enormous hard-on

LEAVING MT. BALDY

I came down from the mountain
after many years of study
and rigorous practice.
I left my robes hanging on a peg
in the old cabin
where I had sat so long
and slept so little.
I finally understood
I had no gift
for Spiritual Matters.
'Thank You, Beloved'
I heard a heart cry out
as I entered the stream of cars
on the Santa Monica Freeway,
westbound for L.A.
A number of people
(some of them practitioners)
have begun to ask me angry questions
about The Ultimate Reality.
I suppose it's because
they don't like to see
old Jikan smoking.

– 1999

Dear Roshi,
I'm sorry that I cannot
help you now, because
I met this woman.

Please forgive my
selfishness.

I send you
Birthday Greetings,
deep affection and
respect.

Jikan
the useless monk
bows his head

Then a lot of things happened. I was struck on the head by an atheist. I never recovered my sense of confidence. Even today I am frightened by the smallest things. Old Mother Hubbard moved into the wound and produced her brood. For many years my head was laced up. I pretended to help everyone.

I sobered up. I faced my misery. Pine trees appeared, grey mountains, misty vistas in the early morning, people with interesting lives. G-d, your life is interesting, I never stopped saying. I never stopped shaking my head in convivial disbelief.

There's so much I want to tell you. I'm the luckiest man in the world. I learned to skin a rabbit with very few incisions and a lot of elbow grease. Easter is my big season. The whole thing comes off in one swoop and you stuff it with Kleenex and sell it.

Saturday night really is, as they say, 'the loneliest night of the week.' I hunker down with my radio and a few balls of twine, in case I want to tie something up. I let the cabin get very cold and I rejoice in my good fortune. Sometimes a spider will descend on its hideous wet thread and threaten my hard-earned disinterest.

My advice is highly valued. For instance, don't piss on a large pine cone. It may not be a pine cone. If you are not clear about which spiders are poisonous, kill them all. The daddy longlegs is not a true spider: it actually belongs to the Seratonio crime family. Although insects value their lives, and even though their relentless industry is an example for all of us, they rarely have a thought about death, and when they do, it is not accompanied by powerful emotions, as it is with you and me. They hardly discriminate between life and death. In this sense they are like mystics, and like mystics, many are poisonous. It is difficult to make love to an insect, especially if you are well endowed. As for my own experience, not one single insect has ever complained. If you are not sure which mystics are poisonous, it is best to kill the one you come across with a blow to the head using a hammer, or a shoe, or a large old vegetable, such as a petrified giant daikon radish.

– *Mt. Baldy, 1997*

THE PARTY WAS OVER THEN TOO

When I was about fifteen
I followed a beautiful girl
into the Communist Party of Canada.
There were secret meetings
and you got yelled at
if you were a minute late.
We studied the McCarran Act
passed by the stooges in Washington
and the Padlock Law
passed by their lackeys in colonized Quebec;
and they said nasty shit
about my family
and how we got our money.
They wanted to overthrow
the country that I loved
(and served, as a Sea Scout).
And even the good people
who wanted to change things,
they hated them too
and called them social fascists.
They had plans for criminals
like my uncles and aunties
and they even had plans
for my poor little mother
who had slipped out of Lithuania
with two frozen apples
and a bandana full of monopoly money.
They never let me get near the girl
and the girl never let me get near the girl.
She became more and more beautiful
until she married a lawyer
and became a social fascist herself
and very likely a criminal too.
But I admired the Communists

for their pig-headed devotion
to something absolutely wrong.
It was years before I found
something comparable for myself:
I joined a tiny band of steel-jawed zealots
who considered themselves
the Marines of the spiritual world.
It's just a matter of time:
We'll be landing this raft
on the Other Shore.
We'll be taking that beach
on the Other Shore.

THIS IS IT

This is it
I'm not coming after you
I'm going to lie down for half an hour
This is it
I'm not going down
on your memory
I'm not rubbing my face in it any more
I'm going to yawn
I'm going to stretch
I'm going to put a knitting needle
up my nose
and poke out my brain
I don't want to love you
for the rest of my life
I want your skin
to fall off my skin
I want my clamp
to release your clamp
I don't want to live
with this tongue hanging out
and another filthy song
in the place
of my baseball bat
This is it
I'm going to sleep now darling
Don't try to stop me
I'm going to sleep
I'll have a smooth face
and I'm going to drool
I'll be asleep
whether you love me or not

This is it
The New World Order
of wrinkles and bad breath
It's not going to be
like it was before
eating you
with my eyes closed
hoping you won't get up
and go away
It's going to be something else
Something worse
Something sillier
Something like this
only shorter

THIS ISN'T CHINA

Hold me close
and tell me what the world is like
I don't want to look outside
I want to depend on your eyes
and your lips
I don't want to feel anything
but your hand
on the old raw bumper
I don't want to feel anything else
If you love the dead rocks
and the huge rough pine trees
     Okay I like them too
Tell me if the wind
makes a pretty sound
I'll close my eyes and smile
Tell me if it's a good morning
or a clear morning
Tell me what the fuck
kind of morning it is
and I'll buy it
And get the dog
to stop whining and barking
This isn't China
nobody's going to eat it

     Okay go if you must
I'll create the cosmos
by myself
I'll let it all stick to me
every dismal pine cone
every boring pine needle
And I'll broadcast my affection
from this shaven dome

360 degrees
to all the dramatic vistas
to all the mists and snows
that move across
the shining mountains
to the women bathing
in the stream
and combing their hair
on the roofs
to the voiceless ones
who have petitioned me
from their surprising silence
to the poor in heart
though they be rich
to all the thought-forms
and leaking mental objects
that you get up here
at the end of your ghostly life

– after a photo by Hazel Field

TAKANAWA PRINCE HOTEL BAR

Slipping down into the Pure Land
into the Awakened State of Drunk
into the furnace blue Heart of the
one one one true Allah the Beloved
Companion of Dangerous Moods –
Slipping down into the 27 Hells
of my own religion my own sweet
dark religion of drunk religion
my bended knee of Poetry my robes
my bowl my scourge of Poetry
my final circumcision after
the circumcision of the flesh
and the circumcision of the heart
and the circumcision of the yearning
to Return to be Redeemed
to be Washed to be Forgiven Again
the Final Circumcision the Final
and Great Circumcision –
Broken down awhile
and cowarding
in the blasting rays
of Hideous Enlightenment
but now finally surrendered to the Great
Resignation of Poetry
and not the kind of Wise Experience
or the false kisses of Competitive
Insight, but my own sweet dark
religion of Poetry my booby prize
my sandals and my shameful prayer
my invisible Mexican candle
my useless oils to clean the house
and remove my rival's spell
on my girlfriend's memory –

O Poetry my Final Circumcision:
All the pain was in fearing
and ignoring the girl's voice
and the girl's touch and the girl's
fragrant humbling girlishness
which was lost three wars ago –
And O my love I love you again
I am your dog your cat
your Cleopatran snake
I am bleeding painlessly
from the Final Formless Circumcision
as I push up your dress a little way
and kiss your miraculously
lactating knee
And may all of you who watch
and G-d forbid!
are in a suffering predicament
as I go sliding down to Love –
may you speedily be embraced by
the girlishness of your own
dark girlish religion

she said, "Do you believe me now?"

"worship Me in the forms which remind you of Me"

the girlishness of my own dark girlish religion

SEISEN IS DANCING

Seisen has a long body.
Her shaved head
threatens the skylight
and her feet go down
into the apple cellar.
When she dances for us
at one of our infrequent
celebrations,
the dining hall,
with its cargo of weightless monks
and nuns,
bounces around her hips
like a Hula Hoop.
The venerable old pine trees
crack out of sentry duty
and get involved,
as do the San Gabriel Mountains
and the flat cities
of Claremont, Upland
and the Inland Empire.
Ocean speaks to ocean
saying, What the hell,
let's go with it, rouse ourselves.
The Milky Way undoes its spokes
and cleaves to Seisen's haunches,
as do the worlds beyond,
and worlds unborn,
not to mention darkest holes
of brooding anti-matter,
and random flying mental objects
like this poem,
fucking up the atmosphere.
It's all going round her hips,
and what her hips enclose;
it's all lit up by her face,

her ownerless expression.
And then there's this aching fool
over here, no, over here
who thinks that
Seisen's still a woman,
who's trying to find a place to stand
where Seisen isn't Dancing.

We are moving into a period of bewilderment, a curious moment in which people find light in the midst of despair, and vertigo at the summit of their hopes. It is a religious moment also, and here is the danger. People will want to obey the voice of Authority, and many strange constructs of just what Authority is will arise in every mind. The family will appear again as the Foundation, much honoured, much praised, but those of us who have been pierced by other possibilities, we will merely go through the motions, albeit the motions of love. The public yearning for Order will invite many stubborn uncompromising persons to impose it. The sadness of the zoo will fall upon society.

You and I, who yearn for blameless intimacy, we will be unwilling to speak even the first words of inquisitive delight, for fear of reprisals. Everything desperate will live behind a joke. But I swear that I will stand within the range of your perfume.

How severe seems the moon tonight, like the face of an Iron Maiden, instead of the usual indistinct idiot.

If you think Freud is dishonoured now, and Einstein, and Hemingway, just wait and see what is to be done with all that white hair, by those who come after me.

But there will be a Cross, a sign, that some will understand; a secret meeting, a warning, a Jerusalem hidden in Jerusalem. I will be wearing white clothes, as usual, and I will enter The Innermost Place as I have done generation upon generation, to entreat, to plead, to justify. I will enter the chamber of the Bride and the Bridegroom, and no one will follow me.

Have no doubt, in the near future we will be seeing and hearing much more of this sort of thing from people like myself.

just to
have been
one of them

even
on the
lowest
rung

לאל ברוך נעימות יתנו

MY CONSORT

There is this huge woman,
(O G-d she's beautiful)
this huge woman
who, even though she is all women,
has a very specific character;
this huge woman
who sometimes comes to me
very early in the morning
and plucks me out of my skin!
We 'roll around heaven'
several miles above the pine trees
and there's no space between us,
but we're not One
or anything like that.

We're two huge people,
two immense bodies
of tenderness and delight,
with all the pleasures felt and magnified
to match our size.
Whenever this happens
I am usually ready to forgive everyone
who doesn't love me enough
including you, Sahara,
especially you.

HISTORIC CLAREMONT VILLAGE

I don't remember
lighting this cigarette
and I don't remember
if I'm here alone
or waiting for someone.
I don't remember when
I've ever seen so many
beautiful men and women
walking back and forth
in Historic Claremont Village.
I must have been working out
because I don't remember
how I got these muscles;
and this serene expression:
I must have done my time
reflecting on the bullshit.
Children are pulled quickly
past my bench
but the young are deeply
interested
in the fate
of this unusually bulky presence
in their secret cemeteries,
and they twist around
to look back at me.
The bench says,
"You're going to blow away."
The wallet says,
"You're sixty-two."

The seven-storey
Nissan Pathfinder says,
"Try to put your key
in that silver place behind
the steering wheel.
It's called the ignition."

                        – March 2, 1997

DISTURBED THIS MORNING

Ah. That.
That's what I was so disturbed
about this morning:
my desire has come back,
and I want you again.
I was doing so fine,
I was above it all.
The boys and girls were beautiful
and I was an old man, loving everyone.
And now I want you again,
I want your absolute attention,
your underwear rolled down in a hurry
still hanging on one foot,
and nothing on my mind
but to be inside
the only place
that has
no inside,
and no outside.

BODY OF LONELINESS

She entered my foot with her foot
and she entered my waist with her snow.
She entered my heart saying,
"Yes, that's right."
And so the Body of Loneliness
was covered from without,
and from within
the Body of Loneliness was embraced.
Now every time I try to draw a breath
she whispers to my breathlessness,
"Yes, my love, that's right, that's right."

the face
can be
composed
so as to
never
appear
foolish
but rather
menacingly
unbalanced

41

ALL MY NEWS

1.

I was not meant
to be renown
in the present
market town,

but in the future
some may find
what might be used
to change a mind

from slaughter
in the name of peace
to honouring
complexities,

and thus influence
politics
with deeper balance
deeper checks.

And no one has
to be afraid
when on this Path
the deal is made.

2.

Look on low
look on high,
see with Love's
inhuman eye

not only charge
of opposites
(the broken heart
the healing fix),

but what engenders
every turn –
the leader on her
knees will learn.

And he who's sick
with heavy thought
will cherish it
and fold his cot.

3.

Do not decode
these cries of mine –
They are the road,
and not the sign.

Nor deconstruct
my drugless high –
I'm sober but
I like to fly.

Then quickened with
my open talk,
you need not pick
the ancient lock.

4.

Mystery now,
and now Revealed
I bend to Thee
my will to yield,

and whisper here
my gratitude
for every tear
of restless mood;

Who let me breach
the walls of time
so I could touch
the ones to come

with wisdom that
my parents spoke
(established on an
anecdote),

and shorthand of
the unborn mind
with Graceful effort
all combined.

5.
Undeciphered
let my song
rewire circuits
wired wrong,

and with my jingle
in your brain,
allow the Bridge
to arch again.

YOU ARE RIGHT, SAHARA

You are right, Sahara. There are no mists, or veils, or distances. But the mist is surrounded by a mist; and the veil is hidden behind a veil; and the distance continually draws away from the distance. That is why there are no mists, or veils, or distances. That is why it is called The Great Distance of Mist and Veils. It is here that The Traveller becomes The Wanderer, and The Wanderer becomes The One Who Is Lost, and The One Who Is Lost becomes The Seeker, and The Seeker becomes The Passionate Lover, and The Passionate Lover becomes The Beggar, and The Beggar becomes The Wretch, and The Wretch becomes The One Who Must Be Sacrificed, and The One Who Must Be Sacrificed becomes The Resurrected One, and The Resurrected One becomes The One Who Has Transcended The Great Distance of Mist and Veils. Then for a thousand years, or the rest of the afternoon, such a One spins in the Blazing Fire of Changes, embodying all the transformations, one after the other, and then beginning again, and then ending again, 86,000 times a second. Then such a One, if he is a man, is ready to love the woman Sahara; and such a One, if she is a woman, is ready to love the man who can put into song The Great Distance of Mist and Veils. Is it you who is waiting, Sahara, or is it me?

EARLY QUESTIONS

Why do cloisters of radiant nuns study your production, while I drink the tea called Smooth Move, alone in my cabin during the howling winter?

Why do you mount the High Seat and deliver an incomprehensible discourse on The Source of All Things, which includes questionable observations on the contract between men and women, while I sit on the floor twisted into the Lotus Position (which is not meant for North Americans), laying out the grid-lines of shining modern cities where, far from your authority, democracy and romance can flourish?

Why do you fall asleep when, in order to familiarize you with our culture, I screen important sex videos, and then when they're finished, why do you suddenly wake up and say: "Study human love interesting, but not so interesting?"

Why can't the Great Vehicle, which rolls so merrily through the quaint streets of Kyoto, make it up the switchbacks of Mt. Baldy? And if it can't, is it any good to us?

Why do the irises bend to you, while dangerous pine cones fall from a considerable height on our unprotected bald heads?

Why do you command us to talk, and then talk instead?

It is because a bell has summoned me to your room, it is because I am speechless in the honour of your company, it is because I am reeling in the fragrance of some unutterable hospitality, it is because I have forgotten all my questions, that I throw myself to the floor, and vanish into yours.

– Mt. Baldy, 1998

THE MOON

The moon is outside.
I saw the great uncomplicated thing
when I went to take a leak just now.
I should have looked at it longer.
I am a poor lover of the moon.
I see it all at once and that's it
for me and the moon.

Sweet Time

How sweet time feels
when it's too late

and you don't have to follow
her swinging hips

all the way into
your dying imagination

FOOD TASTES GOOD

Food tastes good
but I'd rather not eat
Touching a beautiful young woman
is a great honour
in this vale of tears
forgive me if I pass on this
or take a rain check
Meditation calms the fevered heart
or so the advertising goes
but it drives me
up the wall
of gossip and breathlessness
Furthermore
I don't want to be a friend to everyone
I haven't got that much time
I'm fasting
I'm fasting secretly
to make my face thin
so G-d can love me
as He did before
I had the slightest interest
in these matters

FUN

It is so much fun
to believe in G-d
You must try it sometime
Try it now
and find out whether
or not
G-d wants you
to believe in Him

we are not
convinced
there has
been any
improvement

BASKET

You should go
from place to place
recovering the poems
that have been written for you,
to which you can affix your signature.
Don't discuss these matters
with anyone.
Retrieve. Retrieve.
When the basket is full
someone will appear
to whom you can present it.
She will spread her wide skirt
and sit down
on a black stone
and your basket will bounce
like a speck in sunlight
on the immense landscape
of her lap.

I believe that
you are standing
in the place
where I am
supposed to be
standing

Montreal
2003

BY THE RIVERS DARK

By the rivers dark
I wandered on
I lived my life
in Babylon

and I did forget
my holy song
and I had no strength
in Babylon

by the rivers dark
where I could not see
who was waiting there
who was hunting me

and he cut my lip
and he cut my heart
so I could not drink
from the river dark

and he covered me
and I saw within
my lawless heart
and my wedding ring

I did not know
and I could not see
who was waiting there
who was hunting me

by the rivers dark
I panicked on
I belonged at last
to Babylon

then he struck my heart
with a deadly force
and he said, "This heart
it is not yours."

and he gave the wind
my wedding ring
and he circled me
with everything

by the rivers dark
in a wounded dawn
I live my life
in Babylon

tho' I take my song
from a withered limb
both song and tree
they sing for him

be the truth unsaid
and the blessing gone
if I forget
my Babylon

I did not know
and I could not see
who was waiting there
who was hunting me

by the rivers dark
where it all goes on
by the rivers dark
in Babylon

LOVE ITSELF

for L.W.

The light came through the window,
Straight from the sun above,
And so inside my little room
There plunged the rays of Love.

In streams of light I clearly saw
The dust you seldom see,
Out of which the Nameless makes
A Name for one like me.

I'll try to say a little more:
Love went on and on
Until it reached an open door –
Then Love Itself was gone.

All busy in the sunlight
The flecks did float and dance,
And I was tumbled up with them
In formless circumstance.

Then I came back from where I'd been
My room, it looked the same –
But there was nothing left between
The Nameless and the Name.

I'll try to say a little more:
Love went on and on
Until it reached an open door –
Then Love Itself was gone.

YOU HAVE LOVED ENOUGH

I said I'd be your lover.
You laughed at what I said.
I lost my job forever.
I was counted with the dead.

I swept the marble chambers,
But you sent me down below.
You kept me from believing
Until you let me know:

That I am not the one who loves –
It's love that seizes me.
When hatred with his package comes,
You forbid delivery.

And when the hunger for your touch
Rises from the hunger,
You whisper, "You have loved enough,
Now let me be the Lover."

THOUSAND KISSES DEEP

for Sandy 1945–1998

1.

You came to me this morning
And you handled me like meat
You'd have to be a man to know
How good that feels how sweet
My mirror twin my next of kin
I'd know you in my sleep
And who but you would take me in
A thousand kisses deep

I loved you when you opened
Like a lily to the heat
I'm just another snowman
Standing in the rain and sleet
Who loved you with his frozen love
His second-hand physique
With all he is and all he was
A thousand kisses deep

I know you had to lie to me
I know you had to cheat
To pose all hot and high behind
The veils of sheer deceit
Our perfect porn aristocrat
So elegant and cheap
I'm old but I'm still into that
A thousand kisses deep

And I'm still working with the wine
Still dancing cheek to cheek
The band is playing Auld Lang Syne
The heart will not retreat
I ran with Diz and Danté
I never had their sweep
But once or twice they let me play
A thousand kisses deep

The autumn slipped across your skin
Got something in my eye
A light that doesn't need to live
And doesn't need to die
A riddle in the book of love
Obscure and obsolete
Till witnessed here in time and blood
A thousand kisses deep

I'm good at love I'm good at hate
It's in between I freeze
Been working out but it's too late
It's been too late for years
But you look fine you really do
The pride of Boogie Street
Somebody must have died for you
A thousand kisses deep

I loved you when you opened
Like a lily to the heat
I'm just another snowman
Standing in the rain and sleet
But you don't need to hear me now
And every word I speak
It counts against me anyhow
A thousand kisses deep.

2.

The ponies run the girls are young
The odds are there to beat
You win a while and then it's done
Your little winning streak
And summoned now to deal
With your invincible defeat
You live your life as if it's real
A thousand kisses deep.

I'm turning tricks I'm getting fixed
I'm back on Boogie Street
You lose your grip and then you slip
Into the Masterpiece
And maybe I had miles to drive
And promises to keep
You ditch it all to stay alive
A thousand kisses deep

Confined to sex we pressed against
The limits of the sea
I saw there were no oceans left
For scavengers like me
I made it to the forward deck
I blessed our remnant fleet
And then consented to be wrecked
A thousand kisses deep

I'm turning tricks, I'm getting fixed
I'm back on Boogie Street
I guess they won't exchange the gifts
That you were meant to keep
And sometimes when the night is slow
The wretched and the meek
We gather up our hearts and go
A thousand kisses deep

And fragrant is the thought of you
The file on you complete
Except what we forgot to do
A thousand kisses deep

SPLIT

What can I do
with this love of mine
with this hairy knob
with this poison wine

Who shall I take
to the edge of despair
with my knee on her heart
and my lips in her hair

So I'll take all my love
and I'll split it in two
and there's one part for me
and there's one part for you

And we'll drink the wine
and we'll hide the staff
and the lover will groan
and the other will laugh

And I'll go to your bed
and I'll lie by your side
and I'll bury the bones
and I'll marry the bride

And you'll do the same
when you come to my room
You'll dig in my dirt
and you'll bury the groom

And I swear by this love
which is living and dead
that we will be separate
and we will be wed

– Mt. Baldy, 1994

if you are young and you don't happen to be Arthur Rimbaud we would prefer not to hear from you

and if you do happen to be Arthur Rimbaud we definitely do not want to hear from you

seal of silence

ALEXANDRA LEAVING

after "The God Abandons Anthony," by C. Cavafy

Suddenly the night has grown colder.
Some deity preparing to depart.
Alexandra hoisted on his shoulder,
they slip between the sentries of your heart.

Upheld by the simplicities of pleasure,
they gain the light, they formlessly entwine;
and radiant beyond your widest measure
they fall among the voices and the wine.

It's not a trick, your senses all deceiving,
a fitful dream the morning will exhaust –
Say goodbye to Alexandra leaving.
Then say goodbye to Alexandra lost.

Even though she sleeps upon your satin.
Even though she wakes you with a kiss.
Do not say the moment was imagined.
Do not stoop to strategies like this.

As someone long prepared for this to happen,
Go firmly to the window. Drink it in.
Exquisite music. Alexandra laughing.
Your first commitments tangible again.

You who had the honour of her evening,
And by that honour had your own restored –
Say goodbye to Alexandra leaving.
Alexandra leaving with her lord.

As someone long prepared for the occasion;
In full command of every plan you wrecked –
Do not choose a coward's explanation
that hides behind the cause and the effect.

You who were bewildered by a meaning,
whose code was broken, crucifix uncrossed –
Say goodbye to Alexandra leaving.
Then say goodbye to Alexandra lost.

– Hydra, Greece, September 1999

these portraits are far behind my actual
development
for instance:
I have
abdicated
the throne,
both the
Temporal and
the spirit-
ual
whereas
on this page
I appear to
be deeply
concerned
about one thing
or another —
this is merely an
old habit of
the face

September
2nd 2003

ORDER OF THE
UNITED HEART

A PUERTO RICAN SONG

'The Devil's Broken Heart'
that was the song
and it was the Devil singing it
and whoever heard that song
would never be the same
and in every heart
of those men and women who heard
'The Devil's Broken Heart'
the weakness weakened
and the Christ of Love strengthened
and people went to bed that night
holding on to each other
like everything else was death
I listened to it
with Armand and Oscar Dorente
and Kathy Hanking
and a lot of other people
I've never seen again

BOOGIE STREET

A sip of wine, a cigarette,
and then it's time to go
I tidied up the kitchenette.
I tuned the old banjo.
I'm wanted at the traffic-jam.
They're saving me a seat.
I'm what I am, and what I am,
is back on Boogie Street.

And O my love, I still recall
the pleasures that we knew;
the rivers and the waterfall
wherein I bathed with you.
Bewildered by your beauty there

I'd kneel to dry your feet.
By such instructions you prepare
a man for Boogie Street.

So come, my friends, be not afraid.
We are so lightly here.
It is in love that we are made;
in love we disappear.
Tho' all the maps of blood and flesh
are posted on the door,
there's no one who has told us yet
what Boogie Street is for.

O Crown of Light, O Darkened One,
I never thought we'd meet.
You kiss my lips, and then it's done:
I'm back on Boogie Street.

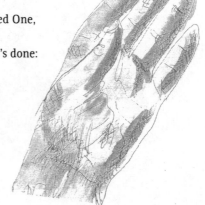

A LIMITED DEGREE

As soon as I understood
(even to a limited degree)
that this is G-d's world
I began to lose weight
immediately
At this very moment
I am wearing
my hockey uniform
from the Sixth Grade

A LIFE OF ERRANDS

If You Are Lucky
You Will Grow Old
And Live
A Life Of Errands.
You Will Discern
What People Need
And Provide It
Before They Ask.
You Will Drive Your Car
Here And There
Delivering And Fetching
And Neither The Traffic
Nor The Weather
Will Bother You
In The Least.
You Will Whip Down
The 405
To San Diego
To Pick Up An Acorn
For Someone's Proverb
And So On And So Forth.
In Spite Of The Ache
In Your Heart
About The Girl You
Never Found
And The Fact That
After Years Of
Spiritual Rigour
You Did Not Manage
To Enlighten Yourself
A Certain Cheerfulness
Will Begin To
Arise Out Of Your Crushed
Hopes And Intentions.

How Thirstily
You Embrace Your
Next Commission:
To Sift Through
The Sunglasses
At A Lost And Found
In Las Vegas
Just A Few Hours
Across The Desert.
Your Hair Is White
You Have Breasts
And A Gut
Over Your Belt
You Are No Longer A Boy,
Or Even A Man
But A Sense Of Gratitude
Enlivens Every Move
You Make.
Yes, Sir, These Are The
Very Gold-Rimmed Pair
She Left In The Plastic Tray
Beside The Dollar
Slot Machines.
No, Sir, I Am Not Lying.

WISH ME LUCK

a fresh spiderweb
billowing
like a spinnaker
across the open window
and here he is
the little master
sailing by
on a thread of milk
wish me luck
admiral
I haven't finished anything
in a long time

MISSION

I've worked at my work
I've slept at my sleep
I've died at my death
And now I can leave

Leave what is needed
And leave what is full
Need in the Spirit
And need in the Hole

Beloved, I'm yours
As I've always been
From marrow to pore
From longing to skin

Now that my mission
Has come to its end:
Pray I'm forgiven
The life that I've led

The Body I chased
It chased me as well
My longing's a place
My dying a sail

RELIGIOUS STATUES

After a while
I started playing with dolls
I loved their peaceful expressions
They all had their places
in a corner of Room 315

I would say to myself:
It doesn't matter
that Leonard can't breathe
that he is hopelessly involved
in the panic of the situation

I'd light a cigarette
and a stick of Nag Champa
Both would burn too fast
in the draft of the ceiling fan

Then I might say
something like:
Thank You
for the terms of my life
which make it so painlessly clear
that I am powerless
to do anything

and I'd watch CNN
the rest of the night
but now
from a completely different
point of view

one of the dolls

WHAT DID IT

An acquaintance told me
that the great sage
Nisargadatta Maharaj
once offered him a cigarette,
"Thank you, sir, but I don't smoke."
"Don't smoke?" said the master,
      "What's life for?"

THE CIGARETTE ISSUE

This is beginning again
and like the first time
the girl's name is Claire
and she's French
But this time
the boy's name is Jikan
and he's an old man

It's not Greece any more
it's India
the new place for unhappiness
but this time
the boy is not unhappy
with his unhappiness
and Claire also has noticed
that the boy
is sixty-five years old

But what is exactly the same
is the promise, the beauty
and the salvation
of cigarettes
the little Parthenon
of an opened pack of cigarettes

and Mumbai, like the Athens
of forty years ago
is a city to smoke in

Well, that's enough for now
I will be able to love her
and also love the rest of my life
from my experience with books

I MISS MY MOTHER

I want to bring her to India
And buy her
Gold and jewels
I want to hear her sigh
For the poor in the street
And marvel
At the unforgiving greyness
Of the Arabian Sea
She was right about everything
Including my foolish guitar
And where it got me
She would make sense of
The cotton flags
The sorrows of the port
The arches of the past
She'd pat my little head
And bless my dirty song

THOUSANDS

Out of the thousands
who are known,
or who want to be known
as poets,
maybe one or two
are genuine
and the rest are fakes,
hanging around the sacred precincts
trying to look like the real thing.
Needless to say
I am one of the fakes,
and this is my story.

MY BABY WASN'T THERE

My Baby wasn't there
When I went to test Her love
But She'll be there today
I pray to G-d above

I'll sneak a look or two
And if I see Her melt
I'll know that it was true
This feeling that I felt

My heart is like a thorn
Hers is like a Tree
My heart is dry and torn
Hers a Canopy

I've been up all night
And all I've got is this
I know that it's not right
But nothing really is

She's there at Her Machine
I'll tiptoe down the aisle
And if it's meant to be
She'll greet me with a Smile

Then I'll be so happy
I'll live another day
I'll thank Her for Her Charity
And then I'll limp away

74

DUSKO'S TAVERNA 1967

They are still singing down at Dusko's,
sitting under the ancient pine tree,
in the deep night of fixed and falling stars.
If you go to your window you can hear them.
It is the end of someone's wedding,
or perhaps a boy is leaving on a boat in the morning.
There is a place for you at the table,
wine for you, and apples from the mainland,
a space in the songs for your voice.
Throw something on,
and whoever it is you must tell
that you are leaving,
tell them, or take them, but hurry:
they have sent for you –
the call has come –
they will not wait forever.
They are not even waiting now.

UNBECOMING

It's unbecoming
to find you
in a place of entertainment
trying to forget
the tiny horror
of the last million years

Most of all
I dislike the brave violin
scraping against
the side of the massacre
as if to infer
that the killers are weak
and the victims will win
It complicates the nightmare
with a dream
It turns the nightmare
outside-in
Discard the violin

And put away your courage
Haven't you noticed
how the thugs
and the blood-drinkers
are drawn to your courage
It is a provocation
in their sight

Give it back to the rocks
to the mud
to that which supports the mud
End this ugly experiment
with the human heart

Please do not tell me again
about the lonely railway station
where we undressed each other
in a hail of apple seeds

And this voice of ignorant
understanding –
experience the deep humiliation
as the tidal silence
refuses to affirm it

Stand there
in the vanity
of your solitude
Summon the short-lived tears
the shallow laughter
the comforts
that obey your suffering
that embrace your defeat

Stand there
goosefleshed and proud
      high-breasted one
in the erotic rags
of religion

I sincerely hope
we do not have to meet again
at the next amusement

     – 1979

THE OLD AUTOMAT ON 23RD ST.

I wandered into the Automat
Wearing a kind of religious hat
The meatballs were round
And the pancakes were flat
I asked G-d in heaven
To keep it like that

– 1970

Paris again
the great Mouth Culture
oysters and cheese
explanations to everyone

TOO OLD

I am too old
to learn the names
of the new killers
This one here
looks tired and attractive
devoted, professorial
He looks a lot like me
when I was teaching
a radical form of Buddhism
to the hopelessly insane
In the name of the old
high magic
he commands
families to be burned alive
and children mutilated
He probably knows
a song or two that I wrote
All of them
all the bloody hand bathers
and the chewers of entrails
and the scalp peelers
they all danced
to the music of the Beatles
they worshipped Bob Dylan
Dear friends
there are very few of us left
silenced
trembling all the time
hidden among the blood –
stunned fanatics
as we witness to each other
the old atrocity
the old obsolete atrocity

that has driven out
the heart's warm appetite
and humbled evolution
and made a puke of prayer

THE BEACH AT KAMINI

The sailboats
    the silver water
the crystals of salt
    on her eyelashes
All the world
    sudden and shining
the moment before G-d
    turned you inward

DURING THE DAY

I sit here
At the window
Waiting for you
To come jogging past
In your crucifix uniform
You remind me of myself
Perhaps (I wonder aimlessly)
I could comfort you
I love the furrows between your eyes
And the ravages of anxiety
Across your clenched expression
You have the new face
The coming face
The face of no objective experience
And you have chosen the path of muscle
Toward your sorrow
How private you are
In the minds of everyone
I salute you
Brave spirit
Who has swallowed so much
And tasted so little.

my secret drug is death
I take it whenever I see you
and you don't see me

2/11/03

Laughter in the Pantheon

I enjoyed the laughter
        old poets
as you welcomed me

but I won't be staying
        here for long
You won't be either

      – 1985

DEAR DIARY

You are greater than the Bible
And the Conference of the Birds
And the Upanishads
All put together

You are more severe
Than the Scriptures
And Hammurabi's Code
More dangerous than Luther's paper
Nailed to the Cathedral door

You are sweeter
Than the Song of Songs
Mightier by far
Than the Epic of Gilgamesh
And braver
Than the Sagas of Iceland

I bow my head in gratitude
To the ones who give their lives
To keep the secret
The daily secret
Under lock and key

Dear Diary
I mean no disrespect
But you are more sublime
Than any Sacred Text

Sometimes just a list
Of my events
Is holier than the Bill of Rights
And more intense

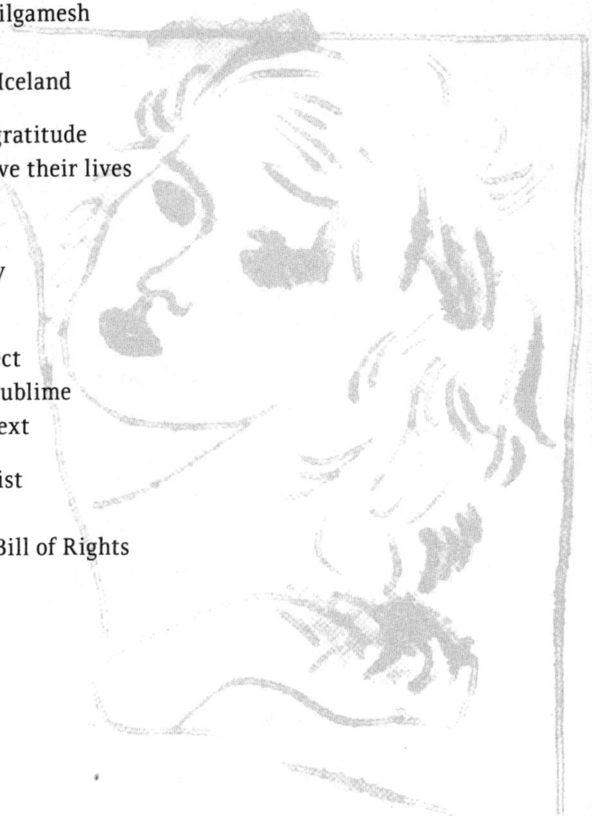

THE COLD

The cold seizes me
and I shiver
The wine
overthrows my tears
The night puts me to bed
and the sorrows
strengthen my resolve
Your name is burning
under a statue
Even when I was with you
I wanted to be here
The rain unhooks my belt
The wind gives a shape
to your absence
I move in and out
of the One Heart
no longer struggling
to be free

A MAGIC CURE

I get up too late
The day is lost
I don't bless the rooster
I don't raise my hands to the water
Then it's dark
and I look into all the spots
on rue St-Denis
I even talk religion
to the other wastrels
who, like me, are after new women
In bed I fall asleep
in the middle of a Psalm
which I am reading
for a magic cure

– Montreal, 1975

the truth of
the line

overwhelms
all other

considerations

1/24/03

LAYTON'S QUESTION

Always after I tell him
what I intend to do next,
Layton solemnly inquires:
Leonard, are you sure
you're doing the wrong thing?

– after a photo by Laszlo

IF YOU KNEW

if you knew how much we loved you
you'd cover up
you wouldn't fuck around
with the passion
that killed three hundred thousand people
at hiroshima
or scooped up rocks from the moon
and crushed them into dust
looking for you
looking for your lost encouragement

I WROTE FOR LOVE

I wrote for love.
Then I wrote for money.
With someone like me
it's the same thing.

— *1975*

LORCA LIVES

Lorca lives in New York City
He never went back to Spain
He went to Cuba for a while
But he's back in town again

He's tired of the gypsies
And he's tired of the sea
He hates to play his old guitar
It only has one key

He heard that he was shot and killed
He never was, you know
He lives in New York City
He doesn't like it though

MERCY RETURNS ME

A woman I want –
An honour I covet –
A place where I want my mind to dwell –
Then Mercy returns me
To the triad
And the crisis of the song.

Jazz on the radio
32 in the desk drawer
Brush in hand
Heart in sad confusion
He draws a woman
The sax says it better
The cold March night says it better
Everything but his heart and his hand
Says it better
Now there is a woman on the paper
Now there are colours
Now there is a shadow on her waist
He knows his own company
The surprises
Of patience and disorderly solitude
Knows the tune
According to his station
How to let the changes
He can't play
Connect him to the ones who can
And the woman on the paper
Who will never pierce the air with her beauty
She belongs here too
She too has her place
In the basement of the vast museum
Not that he could boast about it
Even to himself

Not that he would dare to call it
Some kind of Path
He will never untangle
Or upgrade
The circumstances
That fasten him to this loneliness
Or bent down with love
Comprehend the sudden mercy
Which floods the room
And dissolves it now
In the traditional golden light

My Metal Cup

GOOD GERMANS

You took me to your family
You warned me well before
that your father is a fascist
and your mother is a whore

I was kind of disappointed
I was bored to tell the truth:
your folks they're just Good Germans
but you, you're Hitler Youth

So I'm going to live in China
where you get a better deal
where your killer is a poet
and your comrade is a girl

– 1973

If I Could Help You

If I could help you, buddy, I would
I really would
I'd pray for you
I'd make muscles appear on your back
I'd take you to a bridge
that people think is beautiful
if there were the slightest chance
that you'd like it
I'd get you that motorcycle
I'd put your songs on the jukebox
if you were a singer
I'd help you step across
that crack in your life
I'd die for you on the cross again
I would do all these things for you
because I'm the Lord of your life
but you've gone so far from me
that I've decided to embrace you here
with my most elusive qualities
You always wanted to be brave and true
So breathe deeply now
and begin your great adventure
with crushing solitude

a private
gaze

even though he
was built to see
the world this
way, he was also
built to
disregard, to be
free of the way
he was built
to see the world

THE REMOTE

I often think about you
when I'm lying alone in
my room with my mouth
open and the remote
lost somewhere in the bed

when you rose out of the mist
of pornography
with your talk of marriage
and orgies
I was a mere boy
of fifty-seven
trying to make a fast buck
in the slow lane

it was ten years too late
but I finally got
the most beautiful girl
on the religious left
to go with her lips
to the sunless place

the art of song
was in my bones
the coffee died for me
I never answered
any phone calls
and I said a prayer
for whoever called
and didn't leave a message

this was my life
in Los Angeles
when you slowly
removed your yellow sweater
and I slobbered over
your boyish haunches
and I tried to be
a husband
to your dark and motherly
intentions

I thank you
for the ponderous songs
I brought to completion
instead of ----ing you
more often
and the hours you allowed me
on a black meditation mat
intriguing with my failed
aristocratic pedigree
to overthrow vulgarity
and set America straight
with the barbed wire
and the regular beatings
of rhyme

and now that we are gone
I have a thousand years
to tell you how I rise
on everything that rises
how I became that lover
whom you wanted
who has no other life
but your beauty
who is naked and bent

under the quotas of your desire
I have a thousand years
to be your twin
the loving mirrored one
who was born with you

I'm free at last
to trick you into posing
for my Polaroid
while you inflame
my hearing aid
with your vigorous obscenities

your panic cannot hurry me here
and my panic and my falling
shoulders
our shameless lives
are the grains
scattered for an offering
before the staggering heights
of our love
and the other side of your anxiety
is a hammock of sweat
and moaning
and generations of the butterfly
mate and fall
as we undo the differences
and time comes down
like the smallest pet of G-d
to lick our fingers
as we sleep
in the tangle
of straps and bracelets

and Oh the sweetness of first nights
and twenty-third nights
and nights
after death and bitterness
sweetness of this very morning
the bees slamming into
the broken hollyhocks
and the impeccable order
of the objects on the table
the weightless irrelevance
of all our old intentions
as we undo
as we undo
every difference

the
promise
of a
youthful
shirt

Montreal
2003
Winter

DELAY

"I can hold in a great deal; I don't speak
until the waters overflow their banks
and break through the dam."

Thus I was able to delay this book well beyond
the end of the 20th century.

MONTREAL AFTERNOON

Henry and I
cover our heads
and write a few poems
The prayer book is open
The radio is playing
Henry says: They're not
playing that right,
it should be faster.
The kitchen door is open
It's raining
Henry says: I'm sorry I killed your father
It was a hunting accident
Rabbi Zerkin is speeding
toward us
through the wet city
with the woollen prayer-shawls
that he promised us
on the telephone
Henry says: In the year
sixteen hundred thousand
two hundred and twenty-nine
you will begin a commentary
on the Chumash
and in the year fourteen thousand
four hundred and forty-three
I will begin a commentary
on the Chumash
I'll call mine Tzim Tzimay Ha Yerak
which means
The Contracted Greens of the Greenery;

HENRY'S ARM

then we will write a book together
called Acorns and Other Leaves
                or
The Green Hills of Sunshine
We smoke Players Medium
drink cups of hot water
waiting for Rabbi Zerkin
Henry says: I'm sorry I killed your father
It was a hunting accident
But he'll be back
So will Queen Elizabeth the First

He was kind and powerful. He asked me to read him a poem. And then he asked me for another. And another. This was on the roof of Nancy's house, which she called The Firestation. Nancy gave us lunch, and then I read some more. Later many sorrows befell them both.

NEED THE SPEED

need the speed
need the wine
need the pleasure
in my spine

need your hand
to pull me out
need your juices
on my snout

need to see
I never saw
your need for me
your longing raw

need to hear
I never heard
against my ear
your dirty word

need to have
you summon me
like moon above
the gathered sea

need to know
I never knew
the tidal tow-
ing come from you

need to feel
I never felt
your magnet pull-
ing at my self

now it fades
now it's gone
hormonal rage
unquiet song

HOW COULD I HAVE DOUBTED

I stopped looking for you
I stopped waiting for you
I stopped dying for you
and I started dying for myself
I aged rapidly
I became fat in the face
and soft in the gut
and I forgot that I'd ever loved you
I was old
I had no focus, no mission
I wandered around eating and buying
bigger and bigger clothes
and I forgot why I hated
every long moment that was mine to fill
Why did you come back to me tonight
I can't even get off this chair
Tears run down my cheeks
I am in love again
I can live like this

Voice Dictating in a Plane Over Europe

Leonardos,
I am no longer lonely.
I will accept your friendship now
if you can say
something true about me.
That is correct,
I had a red cardigan sweater
which I used to wear
in the evenings.
The years have brought us together.
Straighten your seat back.
You are landing in Vienna
where I killed myself
in nineteen sixty-two.

THE GREAT EVENT

It's going to happen very soon. The great event that will end the horror. That will end the sorrow. Next Tuesday, when the sun goes down, I will play the Moonlight Sonata backwards. This will reverse the effects of the world's mad plunge into suffering for the last 200 million years. What a lovely night that will be. What a sigh of relief, as the senile robins become bright red again, and the retired nightingales pick up their dusty tails, and assert the majesty of creation!

THE PARIS SKY

The Paris sky
is blue and bright
I want to fly
with all my might

Her legs are long
her heart is high
The chains are strong
but so am I

Things blew all over the place on the day that I was born. It was windy. Dried leaves crashed against the walls of the Homeopathic Hospital. I was alive. I was alive in the horror.

The Givers huddled over me like a football team. They started to give me things and then to take them away. The things that didn't fit they chucked back into the Funnel of the Void. The gifts were many and many were the warnings that went with them.

We are giving you a great heart but if you drink wine you will begin to hate the world. The moon is your sister but if you take sleeping pills you will find yourself in the company of unhappy women. Every time you grab at love you will lose a snowflake of your memory.

My mother was lying not far away and I heard her cry, "He isn't mine!" My noble parent cried to my ears alone from her bed of blood and water. I heard her say it and I thanked her for the truth with a shriek of joy. I was not born into a family. I was fully protected.

The hammers fell on infants everywhere but I was saved on a river in the beautiful autumn land of Egypt.

THE SWEETEST LITTLE SONG

You go your way
I'll go your way too

THING

I am this thing that needs to sing
I love to sing
to my beloved's other thing
and to my own dear sweet G-d
I love to sing to Him and her
and to my baby's lower fur
which is so holy
that I want to crawl on my knees
off a high cliff
and sail around singing
in the wind
which is so friendly
to my feathery spirit
I am this thing
that wants to sing
when I am up against the spit
and scorn of judges
O G-D I want to sing
I Am
THIS THING THAT NEEDS TO SING

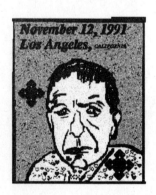

November 12, 1991
Los Angeles, CALIFORNIA

STANZAS FOR H.M.

O perfect gentleman, and champion
of the Royal Throne; O unbroken stone
of Sinai's heart; O Hero of Verdun;
our greatest poet until now unknown,
whose banner over death has always flown
in wilds of poverty and solitude;
I thank you for the years you spent alone
with nothing to hang on to but a mood
of glory, searching words that Love could not elude

(We lost you for a while. The doctors tried
their hopeful science on a chosen soul,
but this chosen soul was sitting by the side
of G-d, and touched by Him, hale and whole,
though broken in men's eyes, in His control.)
O friend who pardoned everyone who came
to light your dark and dim your aureole,
accept this awkward homage to your fame
(nor Modesty supply your instant counterclaim.)

HENRY'S ARM

We do not know the Will or voice that made
you fly from high Decarie's overpass;
we do not know the Hebrew you obeyed
to raise your feet so far from sand and grass
and try the air, O faithful Anabas –
but blessed be the One who saved you there,
and bless His Name, His every Alias,
Who gave you, on that insubstantial stair,
the bravest songs we have of loss and love's repair.

Dear Henry, I know you will forgive these
lines of mine, their clumsy antique tone,
for they are true and not mere obsequies,
and for all their rhetoric overblown
a simple gesture to the man you own,
whose friendship is so rare, whose art so pure,
simplicity is dazed, then overthrown –
alarmed and shy my love must I obscure
behind the fallen grandiose of literature.

I don't know where I'm going any more.
I find myself a table and a chair.
I wait, I don't know what I'm waiting for.
I change the room, the country. I compare
my clattering armoured blitz to your spare
weaponry of light, your refined address –
I know you stand where none of us would dare,
I know you kneel where none of us would guess,
well ordered and alone, huge heart, self-pitiless.

WHY I LOVE FRANCE

O France, you gave your language to my children, your lovers and your mushrooms to my wife. You sang my songs. You delivered my uncle and my auntie to the Nazis. I met the leather chests of the police in Place de la Bastille. I took money from the Communists. I gave my middle age to the milky towns of the Luberon. I ran from farm dogs on a road outside of Rousillon. My hand trembles in the land of France. I came to you with a soiled philosophy of holiness, and you bade me sit down for an interview. O France, where I was taken so seriously, I had to reconsider my position. O France, every little Messiah thanks you for his loneliness. I want to be somewhere else, but I am always in France. Be strong, be nuclear, my France. Flirt with every side, and talk, talk, never stop talking about how to live without G-d.

one of those days
when the hat doesn't help

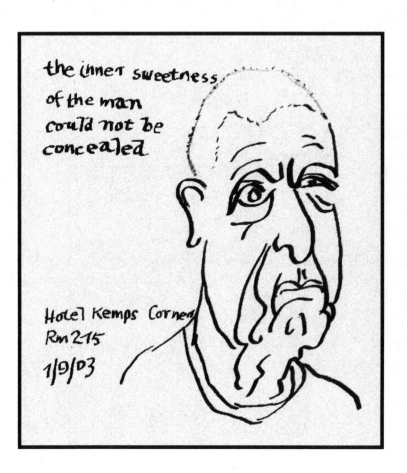

the inner sweetness
of the man
could not be
concealed.

Hotel Kemps Corner
Rm 215
1/9/03

falling
in love
with you

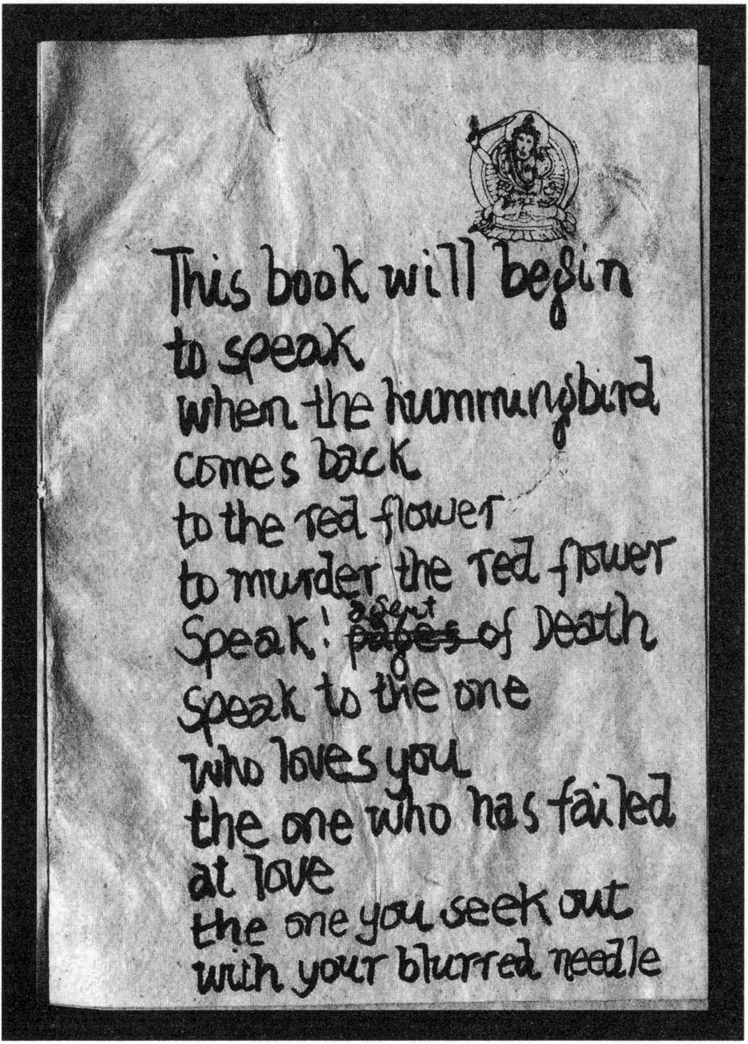

This book will begin
to speak
when the hummingbird
comes back
to the red flower
to murder the red flower
Speak! ~~pages~~ ^{scent} of Death
Speak to the one
who loves you
the one who has failed
at love
the one you seek out
with your blurred needle

119

ON THE PATH

for C.C.

On the path of loneliness
I came to the place of song
and tarried there
for half my life
Now I leave my guitar
and my keyboards
my friends and s-x companions
and I stumble out again
on the path of loneliness
I am old but I have no regrets
not one
even though I am angry and alone
and filled with fear and desire
Bend down to me
from your mist and vines
O high one, long-fingered
and deep-seeing
Bend down to this sack of poison
and rotting teeth
and press your lips
to the light of my heart

MY REDEEMER

I think of you all the time
But I can't speak about you any more
I must love you secretly
I must come to you when I am alone
As I am now
And even now I must be careful
I want all the women
You created in your image
That is why I lower my eyes
When I pass them in the street
You can hear my prayer
The one I have no words for
The name that I cannot utter
I'm twisted with love
I'm burning with boredom
I hate my disguise
The mask of longing
But what can I do
Without my disguise
I wouldn't be created
My Redeemer is a woman
Her picture is lost
We surrendered it
A hundred years ago
"Give us the Lady," they said.
"It is too dangerous now
"to have her likeness on a wall."
So I gave her away
And the language with her
The happy language
She invented for her name
And anyone who wants
To talk about her
Has to become like me
Humiliated and silent
Twisted with love
A specialist in boredom
And other childish matters

FIRST OF ALL

First of all nothing will happen
and a little later
nothing will happen again
A family will pass by in the night
speaking of the children's bedtime
That will be the signal
for you to light a cigarette
Then comes a delicate moment
when the backwoods men
gather around the table
to discuss your way of life
Dismiss them with a glass of
cherry juice
Your way of life has been over
for many years
The moonlit mountains
surround your heart
and the Anointed One
with his bag and stick
can be picked out on a path
He is probably thinking of what
you said
in the schoolyard 100 years ago
This is a dangerous moment
that can plunge you into silence
for a million years
Fortunately the sound of clarinets
from a wandering klezmer
ensemble
drifts into the kitchen
Allow it to distract you
from your cheerless meditation
The refrigerator will go into
second gear

and the cat will climb onto the
windowsill
For no reason at all
you will begin to cry
Then your tears will dry up
and you will ache for a companion
I will be that companion
At first nothing will happen to us
and later on
it will happen to us again

THE CROSS

I am Theodoros
the poet who could not read or write
When I was too old to work
I made religious items
for the tourist shops
I broke down doors
and I put my hands on women
women from America and Paris
They were the ones
who said that I was a poet
I will not tell you about my problems
my son's fall
or my life at sea
I carved crosses
and like everybody else
I carried one
I astonished women with my desire
I fished for them
with goggles and a spear
and I fed them
with what they had never eaten before
If you are a woman
and you follow the shavings
of this man's effort
in the moonlight
you will see my muscled ghost
on the sea road to Vlychos
and if you are a man
on the same road
you will hear women's voices
exactly as I heard them
coming from the water
coming from boats
and from in between the boats
and then surely
you will understand my life
and do a kindness to my soul
by forgiving me
I pray this to the one
who fashioned me out of myself
I confess this
over the wine
to Leonardos
my Hebrew friend
who writes it down
for those to come

— *Kamini, Hydra, 1980*

123

TIRED

We're tired of being white and we're tired of being black, and we're not going to be white and we're not going to be black any longer. We're going to be voices now, disembodied voices in the blue sky, pleasant harmonies in the cavities of your distress. And we're going to stay this way until you straighten up, until your suffering makes you calm, and you can believe the word of G-d who has told you so many times, and in so many ways, to love one another, or at least not to torture and murder in the name of some stupid vomit-making human idea that makes G-d turn away from you, and darken the cosmos with inconceivable sorrow. We're tired of being white and we're tired of being black, and we're not going to be white and we're not going to be black any longer.

Something from the Early Seventies

By and all, or by and large, as you say, the reading public's disinterest in the novel of sensibility behooves itself very well. Or to put it differently, I am very different from most of you, and the older I get, the gladder. I should have come from a different country to entertain you with the horrors of my native land, but I didn't. I came from your very midst, or you could say, your very mist. I am your very mist. But don't be alarmed; you are not in the presence of a verbal fidget. If I strain too easily to push a pun into a profundity, it is only because I am at the end of my tether. I've taken too much acid, or I've been too lonely, or I've been educated beyond my intelligence, or however you want to explain me away. It's a pity if someone has to console himself for the wreck of his days with the notion that somehow his voice, his work embodies the deepest, most obscure, freshest, rawest oyster of reality in the unfathomable refrigerator of the heart's ocean, but I am such a one, and there you have it. It is really amazing how famous I am to those few who truly comprehend what I am about. I am the Voice of Suffering and I cannot be comforted. Many have tried but apparently, and mercifully, I am immune to their shabby consolations. I will capture your tear without hardly trying, in the vast net of my idle prattle. I am going to tell you such a love story that will make you happy because you are not me, but who knows, you may be sobbing behind your ecstasy, as I have hinted, or even promised. I think it's a good story. I think it's tough. I think it's got fibre. I've told it to a lot of people and they all liked it. I'm going to tell it to you. Among my credentials, I am the creator of the Black Photograph. Ask some informed commuter on the subway and he might growl scornfully: Oh yeah, he's the guy who takes a lot of trouble setting up a picture and then holds his hand over the lens when he snaps it. I am truly amused by this fictitious traveller's conversation and I will let his description stand for the process of my art. My art, my eternity. I will be the delight of future eyes when this grotesque parody of humanity has evolved into something no doubt, worse. These future monsters of the unborn seed will pass many excellent vacations of intensity immersed in the emanations of my colourless rectangles. A few years back a clever New York art dealer attempted to capitalize on the most obvious aspects of my eternity, and for a few months I was a figure on Tenth Street, and the darling of a small clique of curiously small and thin people, who were devoted to promoting a "new" form of human expression called ArtScience. Some of these fanatics tried to convince me that they understood what I was doing. Needless to say, they were barking, as was Adam of the fable, up the wrong tree. Nothing anyone has ever said about the Black Photograph has ever meant a fig to me, except, of course, for Nico. She could read them. She knew what I was doing. She knew who I was. And I long for her still. I will pick my way back through the boredom and irrelevance of the last few decades and tell you of a time when I was truly alive, in the human sense, of course. In the other sense, in the realm of the Grecian Urn, in the annals of crystal and imperishable diamond, I have remained the Absolute Creator, life itself to whatever I touched, as immediate, as irresistible, as wild and undeniable as a woman's hand on the adolescent groin. I have been, I am, and I will remain the Ch---t of Matter, and the Redeemer of the Inert. Now you may have an inkling of the spirit in which I conceived for myself the challenge of the Black Photograph. Nico perceived me immediately through all my pathetic bullshit, as some would, and should, call it. My work, among other things, is a monument to Nico's eyes. That there was such a pair in my own time, and that I met them, forehead to forehead; that the Black Photograph sang to other irises, and yes, corneas, retinas and optic nerves, all the way down the foul leather bag to Nico's restless heart, another human heart; that this actually happened constitutes the sole assault on my loneliness that the Eternal has ever made, and it was her.

Therefore I was in New York at a curtain time, in a certain place; actually it was The Chelsea Hotel. This clever art dealer, call him Ahab, possessed the sad misimpression that I would enjoy coming in and going out through a grimy lobby heaped and hung with the fashionable excrement of the ambitious hustlers in the studios above: enormous reproductions of cigar boxes; pillowlike canvases billowing over their innocent frames like so many beer bellies; infantile electromagnetic devices to advertise the artist's acquaintance with technology; mobiles, so badly constructed, that they compounded their capacity for psychic offence with a physical hazard; cognac snifters of various size, painted red and enclosed in a glass cabinet; all in the name of some dreary change of perspective, as if that's what humanity needs; and all these tricks, all these ugly motives, all this poisonous medicine chest of Gotham cunning, promoting itself as the urgent specific to a dying culture; all this profanity made flesh; quickly accumulating layer after layer of viscous grit generated on Twenty-Third Street, and in the low heavens of the neighbourhood; – a presage of the dirty treasure's soon-to-be-unnoticed burial under the sands of time. That's the hotel he put me in. He thought I was one of them. Also Dylan Thomas sailed out from that lobby to pierce his eye on a rose-thorn and hence or thence to assume his rightful overstuffed easy chair in the crowded pantheon of flabby heroism. It can be quickly divined I am no friend of the age.

We will all be airbrushed

we become
frail
and people
see us
naked
who are
forbidden
to see us
naked

25/1/03

BUTTER DISH

Darling, I now have a butter dish
that is shaped like a cow

ARGUMENT

You might be a person who likes to
argue with Eternity. A good way to
begin such an Argument is:

Why do You rule against me
Why do You silence me now
When will the Truth be on my lips
And the Light be on my brow?

After some time has passed, the answer to these questions
percolating upwards from the pit of your stomach, or downwards
from the crown of your hat, or having been given, at last, the right
pill, you might begin to fall in love with the One who asked them;
and perhaps then you will cry out, as so many of our parents did:

Blessed be the One
Who has sweetened
my Argument.

MUCH LATER

Ray Charles singing You Win Again
in the sunlight
twenty years ago
Ray Charles the singer I would never be
and my young wife
'the wife of my youth'
smiling at me from an upstairs room
in the old house
Ray Charles and Marianne
dear spirits of my Greek life
now in the sunshine of every new summer
Marianne coming down the steps
'the woman of the house'
Ray Charles speaking fiercely
for our virgin humanity
Twenty years ago
and again in this Hollywood summer
still companions of the heart
as I measure myself once more
against the high sweet standards
of my youth

— *Los Angeles, 1978*

ANOTHER CHRISTOPHER

There is another Christopher
Guide to Broken Ways
Rejected Christ he carries far
Yours he cannot raise

Separated

I was doing something
I don't remember what
I was standing in a place
I don't remember where
I was waiting for someone
but I don't remember who
It was before or it was after
I don't remember when
And suddenly or gradually
I was removed, I was taken
to this place of reversal
and I was separated
and in the place of every part
there was the name of fear
and for a vast memorial
there was the name of grief
If you know the prayer
for one who has been so dislocated
please say it or sing it
and if there is among the words
an empty space, or among the letters
an orchard of return
please set my name firmly there
with a voice or hand
which only you command
you righteous ones
who are concerned with such matters
But hurry please
for all the parts of me
that gathered briefly around this plea
are dispersed again
and scattered on the Other Side
where the angels stand upside down
and everything is covered with dust
and everyone burns with shame
and no one is allowed to cry out

ANGRY AT 11 PM

you don't want to go out any more
it's bearable alone
just you and the bad news
and the confession of Mother Theresa
God Bless her for letting us know
that she couldn't take it either

2.18.03

THE THIRD INVENTION

Blindly I worked
    at my third invention
taking the chances
    of one who is lost,

feeling my way
    to a cleaner expression
of the absolute filth
    I stumbled across.

And all for the sake
    of an interested woman
riding the night's
    last flicker of hope,

some tourist of beauty
    in full disappointment,
ready to fall in love
    with a ghost.

and here was the ghost
    with his third invention
the usual shit
    for the highest reward;

and now it was ready,
    the third invention,
ready to fall
    in love with the world.

And he falls back
    and she comes forward;
his third invention
    measures them both.

She lies in the arms
    of his third invention
and back in his room,
    he commences the fourth.

This is the work
    of the highest pretension
an automatic ode
    to the world.

O deep in the comfort
    of full employment,
he's lost to the fourth
    and he's lost to the third.

– 1980

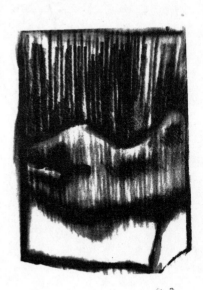

MY MOTHER ASLEEP

remembering my mother
at a theatre in Athens
thirty
thirty-five years ago
a revue by Theodorakis
those great songs
she fell asleep
in the chair beside mine
in the open-air theatre
she had arrived that day
from Montreal
and the play started
close to midnight
and she slept through
the mandolins
the climbing harmonies
and the great songs
I was young
I hadn't had my children
I didn't know how far away
your love could be
I didn't know
how tired you could get

Well, Robert, here you are again talking to me at the Café de Flore in Paris. I haven't seen you for a while. I have several versions of that sonnet I wrote after your death but I never got it right. I love you, Robert, I still do. You were an interesting man, and the first friend I really quarrelled with. I'm slightly stoned on half-a-tab of speed I found in this old suit, it must be twenty years old, and I took it with a glass of orange juice. It couldn't possibly work after all this time, but here we are, talking again. I'm glad you don't tell me what it's like where you are because I have no interest in the afterlife. You're a little pissed off as usual, as if you've just come from something immensely boring. Here we are, talking about the lousy deal we negotiated for ourselves. What are you saying? Why are you smiling? I'm still working hard, Robert. I can't seem to bring anything to completion and I'm in real trouble. The speed is wearing off, or the mood, and I can't tell you an amusing story about my trouble, but you know what I mean. Of all my friends you know what I mean. Well, goodbye, Robert, and fuck you too. Your disembodied status entitles you to a lot of privileges, but you might have excused yourself before disappearing again for who knows how long.

My Mother Is Not Dead

My mother isn't really dead.
Neither is yours.
I'm so happy for you.
You thought your mother was dead,
And now she isn't.
What about your father?
Is he well?
Don't worry about any of your relatives.
Do you see the insects?
One of them was once your dog.
But do not try to pat the ant.
It will be destroyed by your awkward affection.
The tree is trying to touch me.
It used to be an afternoon.
Mother, mother,
I don't have to miss you any more.
Rover, Rover, Rex, Spot,
Here is the bone of my heart.

– after a photo by Hazel Field

SHIRLEY

Let me go back to Shirley
She knew who I was
before the ascension
of sparks
She led me to
the bicycle of armholes
and in her front
I was the glass baseball
of Ancient Greece
the soaring stones
of my mother's mouth
Shirley understood
my straw and my lipstick
the lacquered soda of ambition
and the splash of mind
as it all goes by

She was the
Nurse of Laughter
in the Bat-House
She laughed when
I was born as a surprise
in my father's shaving kit
But enough of you and
you and you
who have captured
all the High Places
I am the veteran
the badge of red
the very friend of Shirley
Return to your
leaves of winter
and your sad jokes
about the reservoirs of
taxation

THE BEST

India has the best Ice Cream
America the best Chocolate
England the best Male Legs
Spain the best Cross
Italy the best Mist
Israel the best Emergency
Canada the best Light
Mexico the best Eagles
Portugal the best Lonely Islands
Egypt the best Minorities
Norway the best Music
Morocco the best Jews
Korea the best Italian Food
I've been to too many countries
I died when I left Montreal
I met women I didn't understand
I pretended to get interested in food
But it was all The Fear of Snow
It was all The Will of G-d
It was all The Heart
swallowing The Other Organs
It was Five Days of Summer
and Two Days of Spring
Mostly it was the Death of my Dog
Sorrow is the time to begin
Longing is the place to rejoice
But I did not begin
and I did not rejoice
I was lazy in G-d
Books lie open all around me
Despite my efforts
they keep coming into my room
And there is a slab of old stone
with cuneiform inscriptions

When I lived in Montreal
I knew what to wear
I had old clothes
and old friends
and my dog had been dead
for only ten or fifteen years
Fortunately there is no Space
        for Regret
in The Poverty
of these Reflections

CLOCKWORK

the crow knows
exactly where to sit
on the yellow bench

the wave
exactly where to break

the jaw that will not
unclench
is fastened perfectly
to the writer's skull

future generations
come like clockwork
under the damp
cement arches

to include themselves
in this well-recorded
afternoon

THE DRUNK IS GENDER-FREE

This morning I woke up again
I thank my Lord for that
The world is such a pigpen
That I have to wear a hat

I love the Lord I praise the Lord
I do the Lord forgive
I hope I won't be sorry
For allowing Him to live

I know you like to get me drunk
And laugh at what I say
I'm very happy that you do
I'm thirsty every day

I'm angry with the angel
Who pinched me on the thigh
And made me fall in love
With every woman passing by

I know they are your sisters
Your daughters mothers wives
If I have left a woman out
Then I apologize

It's fun to run to heaven
When you're off the beaten track
The Lord is such a monkey when
You've got Him on your back

The Lord is such a monkey
He's such a woman too
Such a place of nothing
Such a face of you

May E crash into your temple
And look out thru' your eyes
And make you fall in love
With everybody you despise

NEVER MIND

The war was lost
The treaty signed
I was not caught
I crossed the line

I had to leave
My life behind
I had a name
But never mind

Your victory
Was so complete
That some among you
Thought to keep

A record of
Our little truth
The cloth we wove
The tools we used

The games of luck
Our soldiers played
The stones we cut
The songs we made

Our law of peace
Which understands
A husband leads
A wife commands

And all of this
Expressions of
The Sweet Indifference
Some call Love

The Sweet Indifference
Some call Fate
But we had Names
More intimate

Names so deep
and Names so true
They're lost to me
And dead to you

There is no need
That this survive
There's truth that lives
And truth that dies

There's truth that lives
And truth that dies
I don't know which
So never mind

I could not kill
The way you kill
I could not hate
I tried I failed

No man can see
The vast design
Or who will be
Last of his kind

The story's told
With facts and lies
You own the world
So never mind

THERE IS A MOMENT

There is a moment in every day when I kneel before the love I have for you. Then I remember that I am still that man. And I know that my life's work is to be that man, who leans over a white tablet humbled in his constant and signifying love for you. It is eight twenty-seven in the evening. Once again the thought of you has rescued me from the puzzle of my indifference

and the hard wheel
    in the chest's centre
becomes a soft wheel

G-d lies down next to His lamb
so the creature can
gather itself

His Queen is massaged
by a thousand versions
of Her most devoted drone

and there you are
smiling at someone else
in my vision of the lost kitchen

and that is the way
I finish my work
until it starts again

NIGHTINGALE

I built my house beside the wood
So I could hear you singing
And it was sweet and it was good
And love was all beginning

Fare thee well my nightingale
'Twas long ago I found you
Now all your songs of beauty fail
The forest closes 'round you

The sun goes down behind a veil
'Tis now that you would call me
So rest in peace my nightingale
Beneath your branch of holly

Fare thee well my nightingale
I lived but to be near you
Though you are singing somewhere still
I can no longer hear you

THE FAITHLESS WIFE

after the poem by Lorca

The Night of Santiago
And I was passing through
So I took her to the river
As any man would do

She said she was a virgin
That wasn't what I'd heard
But I'm not the Inquisition
I took her at her word

And yes she lied about it all
Her children and her husband
You were meant to judge the world
Forgive me but I wasn't

The lights went out behind us
The fireflies undressed
The broken sidewalk ended
I touched her sleeping breasts

They opened to me urgently
Like lilies from the dead
Behind a fine embroidery
Her nipples rose like bread

Her petticoat was starched and loud
And crushed between our legs
It thundered like a living cloud
Beset by razor blades

No silver light to plate their leaves
The trees grew wild and high
A file of dogs patrolled the beach
To keep the night alive

We passed the thorns and berry bush
The reeds and prickly pear
I made a hollow in the earth
To nest her dampened hair

Then I took off my necktie
And she took off her dress
My belt and pistol set aside
We tore away the rest

Her skin was oil and ointments
And brighter than a shell
Your gold and glass appointments
Will never shine so well

Her thighs they slipped away from me
Like schools of startled fish
Though I've forgotten half my life
I still remember this

That night I ran the best of roads
Upon a mighty charger
But very soon I'm overthrown
And she's become the rider

Now as a man I won't repeat
The things she said aloud
Except for this my lips are sealed
Forever and for now

And soon there's sand in every kiss
And soon the dawn is ready
And soon the night surrenders
To a daffodil machete

I gave her something pretty
And I waited 'til she laughed
I wasn't born a gypsy
To make a woman sad

I didn't fall in love. Of course
It's never up to you
But she was walking back and forth
And I was passing through

When I took her to the river
In her virginal apparel
When I took her to the river
On the Night of Santiago

And yes she lied about her life
Her children and her husband
You were born to get it right
Forgive me but I wasn't

The Night of Santiago
And I was passing through
And I took her to the river
As any man would do

TRAVELLING LIGHT #31

I'm travelling light
So Au Revoir
I'll miss my heart
And my guitar

It's lovely here
So far away
I couldn't take
Another day

The songs won't come
But if they did
I'd go back home
So G-d forbid

I guess I'm just
Somebody who
Has given up
On me and you

I'm not alone
I've met a few
Who were travelling
Travelling Light

after a photo by Hazel Field

BACKYARD

Sitting in the garden
With my daughter's dogs
Looking at the oranges
And the sky above

Flowers with their shadows
Moving two by two
Listening to the traffic
Hearing something new

Then I start to struggle
With a feeble song
Which will overcome me
Many miles from home

When I Went Out

When I went out to tell her
The love that can't be told
She hid in themes of marble
And deep reliefs of gold

When I caught her in the flesh
And floated on her hips
Her bosom was a fishing net
To harvest infant lips

A soft dismissal in her gaze
And I was more than free
But took a while to undertake
My full transparency

Ages since I went to look
Or she would think to hide
Torn the cover torn the book
The stories all untied

But someone made of thread and mist
Attends her every grace
Sees more beauty than I did
When I was in his place

vibrant,
but
dead

THE GOAL

I can't leave my house
or answer the phone.
I'm going down again
but I'm not alone.

Settling at last
accounts of the soul:
this for the trash,
that paid in full.

As for the fall, it
began long ago:
Can't stop the rain,
Can't stop the snow.

I sit in my chair.
I look at the street.
The neighbour returns
my smile of defeat.

I move with the leaves.
I shine with the chrome.
I'm almost alive.
I'm almost at home.

No one to follow
and nothing to teach,
except that the goal
falls short of the reach.

he's going to get sick
and die alone

he is the main character
in my little story called

The House of Prayer

for all my art

and all my skin

september 15 2003

it never looked like me — never once

155

OPENED MY EYES

G-d opened my eyes this morning
loosened the bands of sleep
let me see
the waitress's tiny earrings
and the merest foothills
of her small breasts
multiplied her front and back
in the double mirrors
of the restaurant
granted to me speed
and the penetration of layers
and turned me like a spindle
so I could gather in
and make my own
every single version of her beauty
Thank You Ruler of the World
Thank You for calling me Honey

The Correct Attitude

Except for a couple of hours
in the morning
which I passed in the company
of a sage
I stayed in bed
without food
only a few mouthfuls of water
"You are a fine-looking old man"
I said to myself in the mirror
"And what is more
you have the correct attitude
You don't care if it ends
or if it goes on
And as for the women
and the music
there will be plenty of that
in Paradise"
Then I went to the Mosque
of Memory
to express my gratitude

NOT A JEW

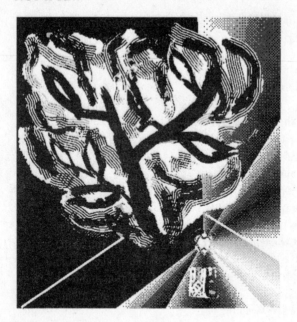

Anyone who says
I'm not a Jew
is not a Jew
I'm very sorry
but this decision
is final

TITLES

I had the title Poet
and maybe I was one
for a while
Also the title Singer
was kindly accorded me
even though
I could barely carry a tune
For many years
I was known as a Monk
I shaved my head and wore robes
and got up very early
I hated everyone
but I acted generously
and no one found me out
My reputation
as a Ladies' Man was a joke
It caused me to laugh bitterly
through the ten thousand nights
I spent alone
From a third-storey window
above the Parc du Portugal
I've watched the snow
come down all day
As usual
there's no one here
There never is
Mercifully
the inner conversation
is cancelled
by the white noise of winter
*"I am neither the mind,
The intellect,
nor the silent voice within . . ."*
is also cancelled

and now Gentle Reader
in what name
in whose name
do you come
to idle with me
in these luxurious
and dwindling realms
of Aimless Privacy?

PUPPETS

German puppets
burnt the Jews
Jewish puppets
did not choose

Puppet vultures
eat the dead
Puppet corpses
they are fed

Puppet winds and
puppet waves
Puppet sailors
in their graves

Puppet flower
Puppet stem
Puppet Time
dismantles them

Puppet me and
puppet you
Puppet German
Puppet Jew

Puppet presidents
command
puppet troops to
burn the land

Puppet fire
puppet flames
feed on all the
puppet names

Puppet lovers
in their bliss
turn away from
all of this

Puppet reader
shakes his head
takes his puppet
wife to bed

Puppet night
comes down to say
the epilogue to
puppet day

this mood has
nothing to do
with you

NEVER ONCE

India is filled
with many
exceptionally beautiful women
who don't desire me
I verify this
every single day
as I walk around
the city of Bombay
I look into face after face
and never once
have I been wrong

WHO DO YOU REALLY REMEMBER

My father died when I was nine;
my mother when I was forty-six.
In between, my dog and several friends.
Recently, more friends,
real friends,
uncles and aunts,
many acquaintances.
And then there's Sheila.
She said, Don't be a jerk, Len.
Take your desire seriously.
She died not long after
we were fifteen.

This is the best way to do it
We will be able to write like this
for a long long time
I think you will be able to read it
In fact, I'm sure you will
It will have pictures of me

in colour

LOOKING AWAY

you would look at me
and it never occurred to me
that you might be choosing
the man of your life

you would look at me
over the bottles and the corpses
and I thought
you must be playing with me

you must think I'm crazy enough
to step behind your eyes
into the open elevator shaft

so I looked away
and I waited
until you became a palm tree

or a crow

or the vast grey ocean of wind
or the vast grey ocean of mind

now look at me
married to everyone but you

EVEN SOME OF MY OWN

This is the end of it all
There won't be much more
Maybe a cry or two
From the peanut gallery
Where I have made
My last stand
In the meantime
Operate on the heart
With proven songs
Such as Ave Marie
And Kol Nidre
Even some of my own
And execute
The recommended procedures
Such as kneeling down
Beside the appalling heap
Of days and nights
And patting the newest seconds
On to it
As if it were
A child's sandcastle
Facing the tide
Under a full moon etc.
In other words
Encouraging
In the old penitent
A borderless perspective

oh and one more thing
you aren't going to like
what comes after America

YOUR HEART

I told the truth
and look where it got me
I should have written about
the secret rivers
under Toronto
and the trials
of the Faculty Club
but no
I pulled the heart
out of a breast
and showed to everyone
the names of G-d
engraved upon it
I'm sorry it was
your heart
and not mine
I had no heart worth the reading
but I had the knife
and the temple
O my love
don't you know that we have been killed
and that we died together

WHAT BAFFLED ME

I took pills for my memory
but I could not stop it
from erasing
I had a family once
They could walk on water
There was a one-way chain
that held me to a woman's body
She didn't know she jerked me
every-which-way
But who was she
and who were they?
In the midst of
someone's explanation
I forget
what baffled me

THE WIND MOVES

The wind moves
the palm trees
and the fringes
of the beach umbrellas
The children go down
the waterslide
The grey Arabian Sea
slaps its soiled lace underwear
on the dirty flats
The wind moves everything
and then stops
but my pen
keeps on writing
by itself
Dear Roshi
I am dead now
I died before you
just as you predicted
in the early 70s

SORROWS OF THE ELDERLY

The old are kind.
The young are hot.
Love may be blind.
Desire is not.

back in
Montreal

as for the
past

children
roshi
songs
Greece
Los Angeles

what
was that
all about?

November
18th
2003

ALONE AT LAST

How bitter were
the Prozac pills
of the last
few hundred mornings

stunned
and still
not
suffering

swollen
with
care
and
anxiety

and still
not
suffering

useless, old
and full of
grief, but
still not
suffering

taxes
children
lost pussy
war
constipation

the living poet
in his harness
of beauty

offers the day
back to g-d

Anything which refers to the matter, even obliquely, is far from the mark. An incapacity for relevance is to be discovered as the muscle of salvation, but flexed and exercised as rarely as possible. The economy of desperation must be recognized. We don't need Art that often. Now and then let Her step out of Her underwear. A little goes a long way.

For the moment, the Big Picture (or the Pig Bicture) can be accessed only by means of the Loose Canon (or the Coose Lanon), the Drifting Molecule, the Carcinogenic Radical. Après moi, the return to Classical Proportion. My sanity is a contagion.

Although we have not smoked for many a minute, we are tempted to ask the barman for one from his own pack.

Let us concentrate on the vertigo produced by easing up to the great plate-glass windows, which are all that prevent us from plunging 12 storeys into the Bay of Bengal.

— *The Taj Mahal Hotel*

JANA THINKS OF JOHN

Jana comes out of her house. Wearing almost nothing. The cup is still in her hand. She forgot to leave it on the table. The cold reminds her that she has neglected to dress beyond her underwear and her slip. She turns back. Shivering. Damn you, damn you, John.

She doesn't know G-d has already killed her, and John, and Teri her Persian, and yours truly, who loves her more fiercely than John or Teri, merely because she is a woman. She doesn't know that G-d has killed everyone.

Jana was with me once. When she was younger. When she was experimenting with the old. I want to get to know your body, Jikan. Oh sure. This is sufficiently grotesque, Jana, without my undressing. But she doesn't call out my name as she returns to her unlocked door.

Me, I understand. John, I understand. Jana, I understand, although I hate to lose a naked woman. But Teri, why was Teri killed, as soon as G-d imagined her?

I was one of the things that was put into Jana. Once you have been put in, you have been put in forever. That is love. Sometimes it is greater than Death, sometimes smaller, sometimes the same size.

John has been killed, but that is not why his name is in her throat. It is because she is dismantled in her need of him. It used to be some kind of love but now it is beyond that in the magnitude of pain and dislocation. She has utterly forgotten that she has been killed. Do not comment on this condition unless you've been there.

Still, life goes on. Jana thinks of John, not me. He takes her out to the racing car garage, and she guesses which is his. She is wearing a white sweater which she bought when she was an Italian. (Milan. Mussolini's train station. Kind, grass-stained women I never saw again. All of us killed under the tidal beauty of coming and going.) They kiss. He is off the hook. Her essence is the very leatherness of the bucket seats of his Ferrari.

And over here, my destiny whispers, "Someday in your arms, she will come to understand that she never did anything. And then she will be killed. Many like her will come to you. Many have already come. You have a job. You are a man-at-work, and you have been killed, along with the whole barber-shop, without a hitch."

MY TIME

My time is running out
and still
I have not sung
the true song
the great song

I admit
that I seem
to have lost my courage

a glance at the mirror
a glimpse into my heart
makes me want
to shut up forever

so why do you lean me here
Lord of my life
lean me at this table
in the middle of the night
wondering
how to be beautiful

Room 215
kemps corner Hotel

LOOKING THROUGH MY DREAMS

I was looking through my dreams
when I saw myself
looking through my dreams
looking through my dreams
and so on and so forth
until I was consumed
in the mysterious activity
of expansion and contraction
breathing in and out at the same time
and disappearing naturally
up my own asshole
I did this for 30 years
but I kept coming back
to let you know how bad it felt
Now I'm here at the end of the song
the end of the prayer
The ashes have fallen away at last
exactly as they're supposed to do
The chains have slowly
followed the anchors
to the bottom of the sea
It's merely a song
merely a prayer
Thank you, Teachers
Thank you, Everyone

So Do You

Because you are beautiful, but smelled bad, I knew you had been killed. And you felt the same about me. You said, "You are an elegant old man, but you stink." After the long event of naked intervention, you brought your hands together and bowed. "Thank you," you said. "That was the first time I never did anything." Many are the lovely things I have been told about my luck, but this was surely the loveliest. "How do I smell now?" I asked. "Worse than ever," you said. "Exactly my impression about you," I said. Then you went back to France (or was it Holland?) and we have remained fast friends ever since. Sometimes, when the hummingbirds are still, I can smell you rotting halfway across the world.

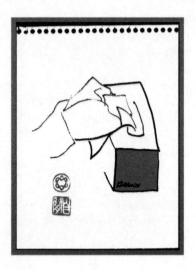

NOW IN MY ROOM

O my Love
I found You again
I went out
for a pack of cigarettes
and there You were
I bowed to everyone
and they rejoiced with me
I lost myself
in the eyes of a dog
who loved You
The heat lifted me up
The traffic bounced me
naked into bed
with a book about You
and a bottle of cold water

THE DARKNESS ENTERS

The darkness enters my hotel room
like a curtain coming through a curtain
billowing into different shapes of darkness
wings here a gas mask there,
simple things and double things
I sit upright on the edge of the bed
and I impede the falling darkness
with my many personalities
just as a high spiked fence
with the tips painted gold
interferes with the French rain
For a number of luminous hours
it is a standoff
Often during this highly charged segment
of my usually monotonous life
a woman enters the room with a pass-key
and in small ways manages to communicate
that we might have lived our lives together
had circumstances been otherwise
I like it especially
when she addresses me in the familiar form
of her incomprehensible language
but always in the back of my mind
I know the important moments
are on their way
and I am that high iron fence
with the spikes painted gold
holding off the inevitable

SUGGESTIONS

"We are college girls from Ontario."

"What part of Ontario?"

"We don't know Ontario. We were told to say we were from there."

"I see."

They moved purposefully around the kitchen, lighting and extinguishing the gas range, checking the pilot lights, extracting pots from crowded cabinets, kneeling in front of the crisper, but no food was actually cooked or served.

"We don't really know how to cook."

"I see."

"We are really nothing but suggestions. Our bodies end where our clothes begin. There's nothing underneath."

"I was wondering about that."

"Yes, we were told to practise modesty, to make you laugh and smile, and not to bewilder you with fluids and nakedness."

"Will this improve the evening?"

"It will. It will delight you."

"I submit myself to your good intentions."

They each took one of his arms, and they folded themselves against him, and pressed their heads against his chest.

"We love you."

His tears came and they wiped them away with their colourful bandanas.

"I'm hungry."

"So are we! Let's go to a restaurant in Montreal, a city, we have heard, which has more restaurants per block than even Rio. We'll go out every night, except when you don't feel like it. Then we'll order in."

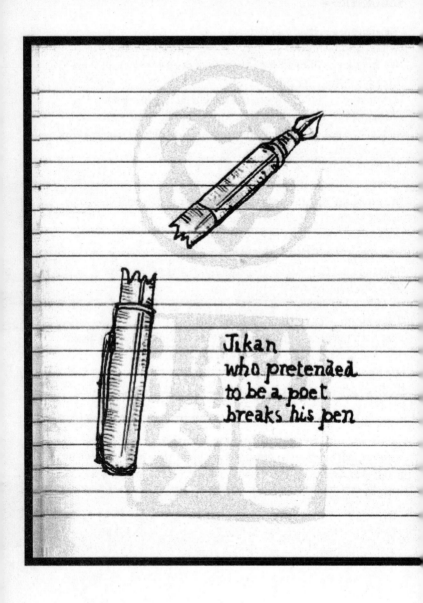

Jikan
who pretended
to be a poet
breaks his pen

EVEN NOW

I did not know
how simple you are
how generous
I tried to capture you
with rhymes
and erotic
suggestions

Even now
you yawn
         in my heart
bored and alone
rubbing ointments
all over your body
and touching yourself
while I tarry

ANOTHER POET

Another poet will have to say
how much I love you
I'm too busy now with the Arabian Sea
and its perverse repetitions
of white and grey

I'm tired of telling you
and so are the trees
and so are the deck chairs

Yes, I have given up a lot of things
in the last few minutes
including the great honour
of saying I love you

I've become thin and beautiful again
I shaved off my grandfather's beard
I'm loose in the belt
and tight in the jowl

Crazy young beauties
still covered with the grime
of ashrams and shrines
examine their imagination
in an old man's room

Boys change their lives
in the wake of my gait
anxious to study
elusive realities
under my hypnotic indifference

The brain of the whale
crowns the edge of the water
like a lurid sunset
but all I ever see
is you or You
or you in You
or You in you

Confusing to everyone else
but to me
total employment

I introduce
the young to the young
They dance away in misery
while I conspire
with the Arabian Sea
to create
an ugly silence
which gets the ocean
off my back
and more important
lets another poet say
how much I love you

PARDON ME

Pardon me, lords and ladies,
if I do not think of myself
as the disease.
Pardon me if I receive the Holy Spirit
without telling you about it.
Pardon me,
Commissars of the West,
if you do not think
I have suffered enough.

HER FRIEND

she doesn't know
her friend has come

she won't be able
to write down
anything he says

he won't have a place
in her notebook
along with Kabir
and the Theravadins

many years later
she will remember
sitting with an old man

a curious nakedness
of thought
between them

that nakedness
that transparency
will lead her home

I guess it's better to start a war
or to stab a rabbi
than to look at yourself
in the mirror of your hotel room
It's better to get carried away
by your culture
	the brave children
	in front of the tanks
	the holy soil
		speaking your language
Shame on you, Great Poets!
I love the past as well as you
but I've got to do something
 to change your stupid bloodthirsty
		music
which no one but G-d really likes
GET BACK TO YOUR DIARIES

It Seemed the Better Way

It seemed the better way
When first I heard him speak
But now it's much too late
To turn the other cheek

It sounded like the truth
It seemed the better way
You'd have to be a fool
To choose the meek today

I wonder what it was
I wonder what it meant
He seemed to touch on love
But then he touched on death

Better hold my tongue
Better learn my place
Lift my glass of blood
Try to say the Grace

THE GREAT DIVIDE

I never liked the way you loved
So devious, so dated
But still I fasted like a monk
And prayed to see you naked

I'd see you hurting everyone
A government of suffering
I'd tell myself 'Thy Will Be Done
My will it counts for nothing'

I drank a lot I lost my job
I lived like nothing mattered
And you, you never came across
You never even answered

It was a blind and broken time
And kindness was forbidden
I guess I tried to hitch a ride
From acid to religion

But every guiding light was gone
And every good direction
The book of love I read was wrong
It had a happy ending

But when the system had been shocked
Beyond all recognition
The simple things that I'd forgot
Resumed their sweet position

I thought I saw you with a child
I thought I heard you weeping
And all the garden round you wild
And safely in your keeping

I don't recall what happened next
I kept you at a distance
But tangled in the knot of sex
My punishment was lifted

Your remedies beneath my hand
Your fingers in my hair
The kisses on our lips began
That ended everywhere

And when I gathered up to leave
You drew me to your side
To be as Adam was to Eve
Before the Great Divide

And fastened here we cannot move
Except to one another
We spread and drown as lilies do
From nowhere to the centre

And here I cannot lift a hand
To trace the lines of beauty
But lines are traced and love is glad
To come and go so freely

And here no sin can be confessed
No sinner be forgiven
It's written that the law must rest
Before the law is written

And here the silence is erased
The background all dismantled
Your beauty cannot be compared
No mirror here, no shadow

But now it comes, a grazing wind
Aimless and serene
It wounds me as I part your lips
It wounds us in between

And now the wars can start anew
The torture and the laughter
We cry aloud, as humans do
Before the truth, and after

I don't know how it's going to end
You always left that open
But oh, you are the only friend
I never thought of knowing

I Am Now Able

I am now able
to sleep twenty hours a day
The remaining four
are spent
telephoning a list
of important people
in order
to say goodnight

Jikan
who was born
to make men laugh
bows his head

this feels good

September 8 2003
Los Angeles

THE FLOW

You have been told to
"go with the flow"
but as you know
from your studies,
there is no flow,
nor is there actually
any coming or going.
These are merely
helpful concepts
for the novice monk.
You can start smoking again,
and what is called "your death"
and what is called "your life"
you can watch now
through the eyes of wisdom.
This is why
the Sages of Japan
named their cigarettes
"Hope" and "Peace"
and "Peace Light" and "Short Hope"
and "Short Hope Light."

A Note to the Chinese Reader

Dear Reader,

Thank you for coming to this book. It is an honour, and a surprise, to have the frenzied thoughts of my youth expressed in Chinese characters. I sincerely appreciate the efforts of the translator and the publishers in bringing this curious work to your attention. I hope you will find it useful or amusing.

When I was young, my friends and I read and admired the old Chinese poets. Our ideas of love and friendship, of wine and distance, of poetry itself, were much affected by those ancient songs. Much later, during the years when I practised as a Zen monk under the guidance of my teacher Kyozan Joshu Roshi, the thrilling sermons of Lin Chi (Rinzai) were studied every day. So you can understand, Dear Reader, how privileged I feel to be able to graze, even for a moment, and with such meagre credentials, on the outskirts of your tradition.

This is a difficult book, even in English, if it is taken too seriously. May I suggest that you skip over the parts you don't like? Dip into it here and there. Perhaps there will be a passage, or even a page, that resonates with your curiosity. After a while, if you are sufficiently bored or unemployed, you may want to read it from cover to cover. In any case, I thank you for your interest in this odd collection of jazz riffs, pop-art jokes, religious kitsch and muffled prayer, an interest which indicates, to my thinking, a rather reckless, though very touching, generosity on your part.

Beautiful Losers was written outside, on a table set among the rocks, weeds and daisies, behind my house on Hydra, an island in the Aegean Sea. I lived there many years ago. It was a blazing hot summer. I never covered my head. What you have in your hands is more of a sunstroke than a book.

Dear Reader, please forgive me if I have wasted your time.

We will not be staying for the entire performance

01/01/04

197

THE FAITH

The sea so deep and blind
The sun, the wild regret
The club, the wheel, the mind,
O love, aren't you tired yet?

The blood, the soil, the faith
These words you can't forget
Your vow, your holy place
O love, aren't you tired yet?

A cross on every hill
A star, a minaret
So many graves to fill
O love, aren't you tired yet?

The sea so deep and blind
Where still the sun must set
And time itself unwind
O love, aren't you tired yet?

HERE IT IS

Here is your crown
and your seal and rings
and here is your love
for all things

Here is your cart
your cardboard and piss
and here is your love
for all of this

May everyone live
and may everyone die
Hello, my love
and my love, Goodbye

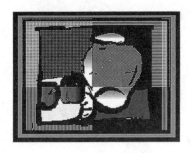

Here is your wine
and your drunken fall
and here is your love
your love for it all

Here is your sickness
your bed and your pan
and here is your love
for the woman, the man

And here is the night
the night has begun
and here is your death
in the heart of your son

and here is the dawn
(until death do us part)
and here is your death
in your daughter's heart

And here you are hurried
and here you are gone
and here is the love
that it's all built upon

Here is your cross
your nails and your hill
and here is your love
that lists where it will

May everyone live
and may everyone die
Hello, my love
and my love, Goodbye

worried
    of course

defeated
    of course

old
    of course

יהוה
grateful
    of course

ever since
the backgroud
dissolved

THERE FOR YOU

When it all went down
And the pain came through
I get it now
I was there for you

Don't ask me how
I know it's true
I get it now
I was there for you

I make my plans
Like I always do
But when I look back
I was there for you

I walk the streets
Like I used to do
And I freeze with fear
But I'm there for you

I see my life
In full review
It was never me
It was always you

You sent me here
You sent me there
Breaking things
I can't repair

Making objects
Out of thought
Making more
By thinking not

Eating food
And drinking wine
A body that
I thought was mine

Dressed as arab
Dressed as jew
O mask of iron
I was there for you

Moods of glory
Moods so foul
The world comes through
A bloody towel

And death is old
But it's always new
I freeze with fear
And I'm there for you

I see it clear
I always knew
It was never me
I was there for you

I was there for you
My darling one
And by your law
It all was done

Don't ask me how
I know it's true
I get it now
I was there for you

A PROMISE

I will never
return
the Holy Grail
to its
"rightful owners."

further-
more,
you do
not have
the
legitimate
authority
to examine me

REPORT TO R.S.B.

Peace did not come into my life.
My life escaped
       and peace was there.
Often I bump into my life,
trying to catch its breath,
pay a bill,
or tolerate the news,
tripping as usual
over the cables
       of someone's beauty –
My little life:
so loyal,
so devoted to its obscure purposes –
And, I hasten to report,
doing fine without me.

IRVING AND ME AT THE HOSPITAL

He stood up for Nietzsche
I stood up for Christ
He stood up for victory
I stood up for less

I loved to read his verses
He loved to hear my song
We never had much interest
In who was right or wrong

His boxer's hands were shaking
He struggled with his pipe
Imperial Tobacco
Which I helped him light

– after the photo by Laszlo

sit still
and let
them
examine
you

February
7ᵗʰ 2005

still looking
at the girls
but there are
no girls
none at all
there is only
(this'll kill ya)
inner peace
& harmony

the evening in the hotel   1/7/03

BECAUSE OF A FEW SONGS

Because of a few songs
wherein I spoke of their mystery,
women have been
exceptionally kind
to my old age.
They make a secret place
in their busy lives
and they take me there.
They become naked
in their different ways
and they say,
"Look at me, Leonard
look at me one last time."
Then they bend over the bed
and cover me up
like a baby that is shivering.

THE LETTERS

You never liked to get
The letters that I sent.
But now you've got the gist
Of what my letters meant.

You're reading them again,
The ones you didn't burn.
You press them to your lips,
My pages of concern.

I said there'd been a flood.
I said there's nothing left.
I hoped that you would come.
I gave you my address.

Your story was so long,
The plot was so intense,
It took you years to cross
The lines of self-defence.

The wounded forms appear:
the loss, the full extent;
and simple kindness here,
the solitude of strength.

You walk into my room.
You sit there at my desk,
Begin your letter to
The one who's coming next.

only one thing
made him happy
and now that
it was gone
everything
made him happy

September 27, 2004
Montréal

KITCHEN TABLE

The same useless thoughts arise
but no one claims them –
Loneliness seizes the frame
and shakes away hope
but no one is hopeless
no one is lonely –
The intricate preparations
for the next moment
direct you
to read this now –
Surrendered to the One
who placed me here
I sit at the very table
where these songs began
some forty years ago –
busy as a bee
in the solitude

– Hydra, 1999

GRAVITY

I never tried to see your face,
Nor did I want to know
The details of some lower place
Where I would have to go.

But love is strong as gravity,
And everyone must fall.
At first it's from the apple tree,
And then the western wall.

At first it's from the apple tree,
And then the western wall.
And then from you and then from me
And then from one and all

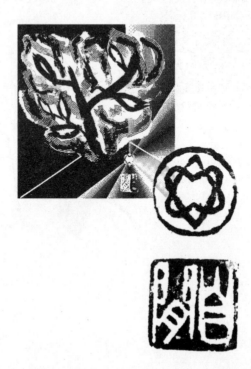

THE SUN

I've been to the sun
It's nothing special
A place of violence
Much like our own

The sun said
I am an open book
Be patient

You will find
That everything happens
The same way
Here and there

The solar winds
Are something else
No one masters them
No one really
Navigates them

You survive them
Or you are never
Heard from again

I love the way
The sun speaks
It is so calm and honest
Except when seized
By its own misfortunes

Soon there will be no one to draw me as I am not O mysterious imprecision of my art

the road
is too long
the sky
is too vast
the wandering
heart
is homeless
at last

GO LITTLE BOOK

Go little book
And hide
And be ashamed
Of your irrelevance

A fluke
Has made you prominent
You were meant
To be discovered
Later

When there are no more
Floods and earthquakes
And holy wars

Go little book
And stop disgracing me
There are serious men
And women in my life
And you have given them
The upper hand

Hide behind
A window
O my dear lighthearted
And transparent
Book
Or crush yourself
Beneath a defeat

But hide
Hide quickly now
And let me hear from you
In our secret code
Which resembles
A bad cough

That dark rattle
Which ignores
The challenges of love
The crystals of perfection

O speak to me
From places
You will find

Go little book
Invite me there

HOSPITALITY

drinking cognac
with the old man –
        his exquisite hospitality
in the shack by the river –
that is, no hospitality
just emptying the bottle into my glass
and filling my plate
and falling asleep
when it was time to go

THE CENTRE

When I am at the centre
of my unrequited love
I cannot hold it as an object
It has no sharp edges
to torture anyone
I breathe the fragrance
of the longing
and the longing
has no proprietor
"O my love" embraces
the great wide sky
as the night picks through
the constellations
lifting necklace
after dripping necklace
for the delight
of Leonard's true beloved
"O my love" cries out
from every pore of snow
and the forest answers
from a great height:
"O my love"
And one heart appears
and one heart dissolves
and they clasp in the place
where I am held up
in the storm
And I walk to you
on the waves of desire
walk across the distance
with something new to tell you
about your beauty
your good legs
and your relentless absence

YOUR RELENTLESS APPETITE
FOR NEW PERSPECTIVES

When You wanted
to see her
in a different light
You placed her
in my arms

When You wanted
to vanish
in a sigh of relief
You drew down her lips
to mine

O Nameless Subject
of all activity
You have given me a song
for my ghostly life

How deep is Your longing
for Yourself
how sublimely overlooked

We kneel in gratitude
as the movements in love
disperse our sweet intentions
across the fictions
of Companionship –
two of the creatures
which You named Me

BETTER TO BE LOST

It is better when I'm lost
and the towns flow by
like television
and you want to be an artist
and draw the waitress's lips

It is better when I wake up
alone in the cold sauna
and get to know the wood again
the red wood, the cedar
the old oaken bucket
the old rugged cross

O my children it is better
to be lost when you are
this poisoned father
at the woman's banquet of love
and I did not take you
to hunt the bear
or spear the fish
I did not spirit you away
from the intrigue
to the forest green
where I slept with
a person named Sahara
beside The Devil's River

and I knew how to put up
a tent in the wind

It is better to be lost
to fall asleep according
to the terrors of CNN
dead drunk on red wine
digging for the sunlight
in the German documentary
that never turns into English

It is better to be the blood
inside my own hand
with its own sweet life
its innocent joyous burden
of service
O thank you dear sweet
loyal blood of my hand
I promise never to raise you
again in anger

INSIDE OUR LOVE

I want to love you now
I want to love you then
I want to love you never
And then begin again

All the tassels of my belt
Go flying in the sky
When you bend down to laugh at me
From your place on high

I want to be the fool
The one you send away
After you have used him up
Every second day

I want to be the rose
You beckon with a yawn
Limping on a thorny crutch
Across the burning lawn

See what you have done to me
As if you give a shit
I used to live behind a line
But now I'm over it

I won't come back to say goodbye
I'll never leave your side
Until I am the other man
And you are someone's bride

Sit down on my memory
When you are in pain
When you are in pleasure
Sit down on it again

Thank you for your courtesy
And for your drunken kiss
I'm drunker than you'll ever be
I hate to tell you this

And every night's cemented tight
Until you strike and rise
Against me like a tidal flood
To crack the wall of lies

And push me down forever
To places where I find
The fossils of my brotherhood
The smooth ones and the spined

And then a holy moment comes
With crisp sobriety:
I see that we are meant for chains
Though every atom's free

I see that we are meant for chains
Tho' every atom's free
And even beauty meets an edge
As one can plainly see

Then summer has your golden hair
And autumn has your ghost
And we are at a juicy feast
Where no one is the host

Then we begin to form again
It takes a little while
I circle round your privacy
For many a lonesome mile

I copied time
I knew I was a fiction
but I could not suspend myself

Moving back
or going forward
I encountered
no obstacles

I carried mountains
leaves fell inside me

I surrounded
your beauty
with applause

and when
you wanted to go home
I swept aside the infant dust

but turn me on my side
so I can better see
that dear expanse
of grassy lawn
where on she
walked, or
should I
say,
floated,

yes, floated
under the
sunfilled
sail of her parasol   2/4/03

THE LAMP IN ROOM 3

CURIOUS, was it not?
it fell on me to
proclaim, from this hotel

Hotel Ste. Anne beside
the **LUBERON**,
the end of human solitude
I find it curious

who ever thought
that I would be the
one to proclaim

the end of human
solitude from this hotel
human solitude
from this hotel

the sweetest duty
to proclaim
the news that I
myself
was waiting for
the end of human soli
Of human solitude

1980

HALF THE WORLD

Every night she'd come to me
I'd cook for her, I'd pour her tea
She was in her thirties then
had made some money, lived with men
We'd lay us down to give and get
beneath the white mosquito net
And since no counting had begun
we lived a thousand years in one
The candles burned, the moon went down
the polished hill, the milky town
transparent, weightless, luminous,
uncovering the two of us
on that fundamental ground,
where love's unwilled, unleashed, unbound
and half the perfect world is found

Montreal
November
19th
2003

pretending to dig in

CHEATER

I cheat when I make love
She thinks it's great
She shows me stuff
that you'd only show
to a cheater

THE FLOOD

The flood it is gathering
Soon it will move
Across every valley
Against every roof
The body will drown
And the soul will break loose
I write all this down
But I don't have the proof

– Sinai, 1973

Index of Titles / *drawings, first lines*

Acknowledgments

Many of these poems and drawings first appeared in The Leonard Cohen Files (www.leonardcohenfiles.com), a remarkable website out of Finland mastered by Jarkko Arjatsalo, with the technical assistance of his son Rauli. I am deeply grateful to the Arjatsalo family, and to the webmasters Marie Mazur, Tomislav Sakic, and Patrice Clos for their extraordinary efforts on behalf of my work.

Some of the pieces in this book became lyrics for songs that Sharon Robinson and I wrote and sang together. They can be heard on the Sony CD called *Ten New Songs*.

The *Walrus* magazine, out of Toronto, graciously published some poems and drawings, as did *Oris*, out of Zagreb, with Croatian translations.

I heard many interesting and precise ideas, which later I blurred into verse, while in the precious company of Kyozan Joshu Roshi, and Ramesh S. Balsekar. Their compelling concepts were so imperfectly grasped that I cannot be accused either of stealing or absorbing them.

I thank my editors in Toronto and New York, Ellen Seligman and Dan Halpern, for the wide hospitality of their houses, and Marilyn Biderman of M&S for carefully presenting this book to publishers elsewhere.
I thank Sam Feldman, Steve Macklam and Michelle Findlay for helping me across the street.

I thank Adam and Lorca Cohen and Jessica Murphy for their Sabbath company.
I thank my sister Esther Cohen for her exuberant support.

I want to express my gratitude to Robert Kory, Michelle Rice, and Anjani Thomas for their loyalty and their kind and skilful navigations.

And to Anjani, again.

Thank you, Teachers
Thank you, Everyone